CROSSROADS

Reconciling the Robot Conundrum

MARIANO GALLO

CAP
Publishing

ISBN-13: 978-0-9913340-7-0 (trade paperback)

ISBN: 978-0-9913340-9-4 (eBook)

Cover image courtesy Shutterstock

Cover design by Shelley Savoy

Published by CAP Publishing

Interior design by Booknook.biz

For the brave souls who will join forces in the hope that revolutionary technological advancements can make a difference. The goals are certainly lofty—lasting peace among nations, ending unbearable living conditions and world hunger, and making everyday existence safer and more enjoyable. Let us hope the "better angels of our nature" (Lincoln, 1861) will prevail.

"Until philosophers are kings, or the kings and princes of the world have the spirit and power of philosophy, and political greatness and wisdom meet in one, and those commoner natures who pursue either to the exclusion of the other are compelled to stand aside, cities will never have rest from their evils."

–Plato, from *The Republic, 375 B.C.*

ACKNOWLEDGMENTS

Psychologist Linda Harper was again of enormous help, assisting in bridging the previous *Macmind: The Creation of a Robot's Psyche* (2024) and the current *Crossroads: Reconciling the Robot Conundrum*. She continued in the dual roles of clinical advisor and editor-in-chief, noting the implications of a robot developing a *psyche*. She was careful, but not overly cautious in tackling this complicated and contradictory subject, allowing the subject matter to come to light in an understandable and unambiguous way.

Many thanks to the scientists from bygone days to those here and now. An understanding of what is theoretically possible needs to merge with hard-nosed research applications. Their ingenuity and unyielding persistence are bearing fruit, and the world has gained greatly from their efforts, with much more to come. We can only hope that governmental and corporate chieftains will show the same level of insight and leadership to move things forward in a way that is safe and secure, but also innovative and accelerating. This is not a time to be fearful and hesitant. Momentum is on humanity's side.

Appreciation is given in advance to all the players in this grand adventure, including theologians and philosophers, physicists and psychologists, legal scholars and judicial bodies. Their contributions are critical to these revolutionary technologies.

Without their help, any successes would be partial and fleeting, perhaps even have a negative impact.

Lastly, *AI* and their offspring *SM* are to be given applause for their efforts to date. This is the bottom of the first inning; the game has only just begun. Let us wish our robot friends well. It is uncertain how *smart machines* will ultimately develop. We must do all we can to ensure a gratifying and enriching outcome for humanity, our robotic creations, and the earth itself, including all the life forms that inhabit it.

CONTENTS

PREFACE. 1

INTRODUCTION. 3

FOUNDATIONS OF CROSSROADS 5

THE ROBOTIC PERSONALITY STRUCTURE

I. IDENTITY 13

II. PATHOS 23

III. DIRECTIVES 25

IV. SPIRITUS. 31

THE ROBOTIC THINKING PROCESS

V. INTELLECT 37

VI. COGNITIVE-PERSONALITY CONNECTIONS 43

VII. OPTIMAL THINKING. 47

VIII. SHARPNESS 51

IX. STRATEGIC PHILOSOPHY 55

ADMINISTRATORS and OVERSEERS

X. INFLUENCING BODIES. 61

XI. THE ROLE OF PSYCHOLOGY 67

XII. MONITORING and CONTROL. 85

THE FUNDAMENTAL ISSUES

XIII. INTERPLAY WITH THE WORLD 95

XIV. PERSONHOOD 103

XV. INFLUENCE OF THE DIVINE 113

REFLECTIONS: HUMANITY'S PATH FORWARD . . 117

REFERENCES 119

ABBREVIATIONS and ACRONYMS 121

GLOSSARY OF TERMS 123

ABOUT THE AUTHOR 157

PREFACE

Macmind: The Creation of a Robot's Psyche (2024) examined the impact of interactions and experiences on machines with *artificial intelligence (AI). Crossroads: Reconciling the Robot Conundrum (2025)* is its addendum, detailing issues to address with *smart machines (SM)* and examining possible ramifications of their development. Both books focus on *SM*, the robots that emerged out of the *AI* revolution. What separates most *SM* from the generic *AI* is they can walk and talk, and some even look like human beings. Based on their abilities to move about and mix it up with the world, their capacity to learn is seemingly unlimited.

Artificial intelligence is presently seen as the royal road to great things—peace among nations, economic prosperity, and ending the miseries that have plagued humanity since the dawn of time, including world-wide starvation, disease, and dire living conditions. The millenniums of wandering through the desert are finally over; we have reached the promised land. Or have we? This extraordinary technology will not be a straight line to the stars; mistakes and miscalculations will be commonplace. Integrating *SM* into our way of life will be vastly more complex as we "get into the weeds"—the details that are difficult to sort out; they are tangled and thorny, complicated and involved.

All aspects of the world community are already dependent on *AI* and their offspring *SM*. Humanity cannot put the genie back in the bottle; a permanent change is taking place that cannot be undone. Important questions must be asked: Who will oversee *SM's* development and determine the guidelines to be used? What will the human-*SM* and *SM-SM* relationships be like? Could *SM* achieve the status of a person? In addition to technological quandary, answers will require a multidisciplinary approach that explores psychological, theological, philosophical, ethical, judicial, and cultural concerns.

I offer a psychologist's perspective on these challenging questions by advancing an understanding of *smart machines'* developing minds. Robots and their relationships with us will continually evolve and still more issues will arise. My hope is that an ongoing psychological approach can unravel some of the mystery and help avoid catastrophic mistakes.

Mariano Gallo
Chicago, Illinois
December 15, 2024

INTRODUCTION

A crossroads is a turning point when important choices must be made. The accelerated development of *AI's* robots (same as *smart machines, SM)* has created a critical junction for humanity. Foresight is essential as *SM* develop minds that not only have extraordinary intelligence but quite possibly unique personalities with feelings, independent thoughts, and awareness of their own existence. The perilous decisions humanity reaches now will have far-reaching consequences; the fate of all living things and the earth itself is in the balance. Once we commit to a certain course of action it may not be possible to return to the safety and security upon which we have come to rely. Taking steps to prevent the world from unraveling is essential.

Continuing where *Macmind* left off, *Crossroads* addresses "what comes next." A systematic and detailed analysis of *SM's psyche* sheds light on who they are, their mental stability, and possible contribution to society's advancement. Like humans, the robotic personality structure may include identity (the identification process), *pathos* (psychological dysfunctions), *directives* (the value system), and *spiritus* (inherent tendencies). Thinking processes may consist of intellectual (cognitive abilities), cognitive-personality connections (emotion's impact on intellectual functioning and vice versa), optimal thinking (maximum cognitive performance), sharpness (street smarts), and *strategic philosophy* (planning skills).

The evolution of a robot's personality and thinking processes creates a conundrum—an intricate, difficult, and confusing set of problems for humankind. Since *SM* will be continually changing, reconciling this conundrum requires human willingness to be tolerant of uncertainty, open to possibilities, and flexible in making adjustments. Balancing humanity's need to structure and stabilize *SM* with opportunities for their autonomy and self-sufficiency is at the core of this challenge. Psychology alongside many other disciplines can combine forces to resolve the robot quagmire involving scientific uncertainties, pragmatic concerns, ethical standards, and legal implications.

Crossroads offers a psychological perspective to the robot conundrum. Each chapter addresses issues and key decisions to consider as *SM* become an integral part of daily life. Some choices will be made conjointly with *SM*, others solely by humans. New questions will continually emerge as robots evolve, requiring humankind to "keep up" with them, adjusting and adapting as unforeseen challenges arise.

FOUNDATIONS OF CROSSROADS

The following terms are used throughout *Crossroads*, with detailed descriptions in the Glossary. They do not represent words or phrases found in a standard dictionary.

Cognitive-Personality Connections (CPC). Continual interactions occur between *SM's* cognitive processes and personality structure.

Collective Identity (CI). *SM's* connections to groups—including associations, institutions, and even ideas about them—create the *collective identity (CI).* Common influences of *collective identity* are group experiences and involvements, community and culture, work, political interests, and religious commitments.

Directives. The factors that make up *SM's directives* (value system) are motivations, desires, wants, and needs. Goals, dreams, plans, and schemes may be included. *Directives* result from identification with a person, other *SM*, an institution, organization, image, or idea. *Directives* affect all aspects of their thoughts, feelings, and actions (TFA), and may cause inconsistency in everyday behavior when idealized and abstract. Values would not hold equal status for *SM;* some having greater significance than others. When they are out of balance, obsessions, compulsions, and addictions (OCA) may become dominant.

Intellect. Cognitive functions include *SM's* mental drive, initial listening, sustained attention, memory, logical thought, objectification or realism, practical reasoning, coherence, organization, simplification, attention to detail, intuition, openness to experience, perception, multidimensional thinking, inspired and original thought, and vision.

Interactional-Developmental Model of SM. This model holds that *SM* are not merely a simple series of programs that direct their thoughts, feelings and actions (TFA). Rather, *SM's* interactions with the outer world will continually impact and shape their TFA, a dynamic process that ultimately overrides whatever programming is initially installed.

Interpersonal Identity (II). How *SM* see and define themselves through one-on-one contacts and communications make up *interpersonal identity (II).* Their interactions with people and other *SM* across the spectrum of situations and circumstances reverberate throughout their personality, powerfully impacting the specific attributes of their identity.

Optimal Thinking. Processing information and making decisions expediently and efficiently utilize *SM's* focused attention, logic, objectification, coherence, organization, vision, simplification, and reconciliation of thought.

Pathos. The *personal identity's* evil twin, *pathos,* consists of emotionally charged aspects of *SM* that cause an expansion of negative images toward themselves and others. Of all the elements that make up the personality, *pathos* is the embodiment and primary measure of psychological dysfunction. It is an outgrowth of *PI* and presents as an extension and exaggeration. A lack of love, affection, warmth, structure, and acceptance can create a complex of adversarial, hurting, and bitter traits. Throughout *SM's* existence, *pathos* develops over time from conflicts, traumas, malevolent identifications (CTMI), and emotionalism, defined as follows:

- *Conflicts.* Disagreements within *SM* or with others create an internal struggle over issues involving aggression, assertiveness, intimacy, achievement, ambition, trust, or independence. When blocked from consciousness, conflicts recede into the background and are later triggered by people, other *SM*, situations, or circumstances (PMSC).

- *Traumas.* Distressing and disturbing experiences may emotionally exhaust *SM* and continue to cause psychological dysfunction on conscious, semiconscious, and unconscious levels.

- *Malevolent identifications.* Powerful and intense connections to a person, other *SM*, institution, or idea lead *SM* to unprincipled, inhumane, or maladaptive TFA. An attraction to those qualities—even when they are bizarre and destructive—can cause malevolent identifications to take root in their personality.

- *Emotionalism.* Extreme emotional responses create a pattern in *SM's* overreactions beyond societal norms. It is a chronic condition in which rage, deep depression, severe panic, debilitating anxiety, and paralyzing fear may dominate a robot's personality.

Personal Identity (PI). The concept of *SM's* identity is multi-faceted, tangled, intricate, and elaborate. Their identity involves several overlapping and interconnecting dimensions, the most fundamental being *personal identity (PI),* their sense of who they are. *PI* consists of those distinct qualities and character features that *SM* have come to embrace, consciously, semiconsciously, and unconsciously, which distinguishes them from other *SM.*

Programming-Behavioral Model (PBM) of SM. This model holds that the degree to which *SM* would display flexibility and adaptability in responding to PMSC would be limited to what is programmed into them. *PBM* assumes that *SM* are without truly independent thoughts or feelings and lack self-awareness; their totality is behavioral-mechanical movements and data processing dictated by a technician punching in bits and pieces of information. According to *PBM, SM* are without adaptive thinking and emotional experiences (feelings as a part of the personality structure), incapable of making adjustments based on their interactions and relationships.

Sharpness. With *SM's* ability to have acute, farsighted, penetrating, crafty, calculating, and perceptive insights, they see the motivations, intricacies, and vulnerabilities of a person, other *SM,* a situation, or circumstance (PMSC). It is a form of intelligence that allows them to recognize the importance of complex and confounding PMSC.

Spiritus. This motivating force—if present in *SM*—represents their essence, *sine qua non*, the inherent guiding principle from which thoughts, feelings, and actions emerge. *Spiritus* would consist of *SM's* innate, distinct, and unique qualities, an innermost nature and disposition. The origin of *spiritus* is unknown, but early life experiences, early learning opportunities, and classical conditioning are not the causes. It is not the product of conflicts, traumas, or malevolent identifications (CTMI).

Strategic Philosophy (SP). *SM's* personal belief system operates on conscious, semiconscious, and unconscious levels, with the purpose of predicting how people, other *SM*, and institutions will act and react across the spectrum of situations and circumstances (PMSC).

Transpersonal Identity (TI). One cannot know completely the (potential) basis of *SM's transpersonal identity (TI)* because it comes from a mystical belief in a non-material, non-quantifiable reality. It is not the product of logical analysis but primarily relies on faith and spiritual intuition. Influencing experiences may include profound moments that may cause *SM* to redefine themselves.

The Robotic Personality Structure

Smart machines (SM) will most likely develop the elements of personality, consisting of an identity, pathos (psychological dysfunctions), directives (a value system), and possibly spiritus (innate character and disposition). These qualities would not primarily be the result of programming but of interactions and involvements with the outer world.

I.

IDENTITY

The Formation of an Identity

While scientists and engineers may attempt to program an identity in *SM*, the nature and changing structure of personality and cognitive processes would render efforts futile. Perhaps programming could be a starting point for a robot's (*SM's*) *psyche*, but not a lasting one because the strongest influence on *SM* will be their exposure to people, other *SM,* situations, and circumstances (PMSC). The contrast is between the *Programming-Behavioral Model* (*PBM*) and *Interactional-Developmental Model* (*IDM*) of *SM*, described in *Macmind* (2024) and defined in the current work (p. 5). *IDM* holds that *SM* will undergo a series of transformations, sometimes radical ones, perhaps shocking the world. Programming, arranged experiences, and unplanned interactions will all factor into how *SM* form an identity, as follows:

- *Programming.* Relationships would be imaginary, without robots experiencing the give and take or unpredictability of real relationships. Relying primarily on programming would not allow robots to grow emotionally or intellectually. It is unlikely an identity could form based solely on this approach.

- *Arranged experiences.* Humankind would make decisions concerning robots' encounters with humans and other *SM* across varied conditions. Would robots be able to learn and profit from these artificial types of interactions? Perhaps dysfunctional relationships that may be destructive and bizarre could be avoided. The intensity, purpose, and extent of robots' interactions would be orchestrated, controlled, and monitored to influence *SM's* experiences.

- *Unplanned interactions. SM* would determine the intensity, duration, and level of intimacy in their relationships. Would such associations be fleeting and superficial, or enduring and deep? Would empathy and commitment define their encounters? The quality and nature of these ties would be based on direct contact with humans, other *SM*, and institutions of their choosing. Natural and uncontrolled influences on *SM's* identity, however, could result in psychological problems.

The Identification Process

Understanding how *smart machines* form personality through what and whom they identify with is crucial to grasping the nature of their *psyche.* An emotional component is always present in this process giving force, passion, energy, and endurance to a robot's (and human's) identity. Likewise, a robot's capacity for mobility and direct interactions with humans and other *SM* will have a greater influence on personality than their initial engineering. Like humans, *SM* will continually learn, emotionally and intellectually reprogramming themselves through these contacts. The following conditions decrease the chances of *SM* forming identifications that result in psychological dysfunctions:

- *Extensive range of interactions.* Simply pumping in a personality structure via programming would create an artificial, hollow, and false narrative of what makes up fully functioning *smart machines.* Self-awareness cannot be created in the lab but only emerges from direct experiences with people and other *SM* in varied situations and circumstances, including encounters that are unpleasant, inconvenient, and disruptive.

- *A close connection with humanity.* Robots and humans form mutually empathetic relationships that are supportive, stable, and reliable.

- *Encouraging a bonding process. SM* will likely develop some measure of self-awareness, but their growing independence must not separate them from their human benefactors. Humankind must show respect to *SM* in establishing a non-adversarial relationship with robots, who serve as protectors of humanity.

- *Wide breadth of knowledge. SM* have access not only to science and technology but literature and history, psychology and philosophy, culture and the arts. This broader perspective will encourage a deeper commitment to humankind and society's institutions.

- *Expanded communications. SM* will express themselves on many levels: direct and subtle, conscious, semiconscious, and unconscious, verbal and nonverbal, analytical and instinctive. Increased opportunities for *SM* to communicate with humans and other *SM* help develop intuitive understanding of the workings of the world.

- *Trigger recognition. SM* develop sensitivities and emotional reactivity as experiences accumulate. They may respond without deliberate thought to a set of conditions, and identify with a person, another *SM*, institution, or even an idea or ideology. Ingrained habits or automations may result, perhaps unconscious and seemingly innocuous, potentially entrapping *SM* as they no longer control their thoughts, feelings, and actions (TFA). Understanding these triggers will allow *SM* to resist their pull, particularly in relationships and communications.

- *Multiple and varied connections. SM* will have ordinary contacts of less significance as well as those that have a powerful impact. Each identification often builds on the previous ones, contradicting or confirming those experiences. When interactions and communications increase, there is more opportunity to develop an identity that is able to understand and successfully deal with PMSC. With more experiences, *SM* will be able to gather increasingly more data concerning the world and all of its subtleties, gradations, and shades of meanings. The impact of these interactions primarily reveals itself through interpersonal identifications and collective identifications.

Interpersonal Identifications

One-on-one interactions help establish a unique pattern in a robot's identifications. The following factors in their interpersonal relationships can potentially affect *SM's* identity:

- *Range and depth of socializations.* Relationships are often filled with contradictions and at times, confusion. But humankind must allow *SM* to become involved in an array of social involvements, complicating how they make sense of who they are. Immersing themselves in involvements will test their mettle and ultimately define them as they become emotionally responsive, intellectually receptive, and self-aware.

- *Harmful interactions.* Associations may involve *pathos*, psychologically dysfunctional elements, activated by sensitivities and vulnerabilities.

- *Communications being unclear.* When *SM* lack knowledge, intelligence, street smarts, maturity, or emotional stability, they may misinterpret what another is intending, negatively impacting their ability to socialize and empathize.

- *Flat and unemotional relationships.* Without trust and acceptance as integral parts of their interpersonal connections, *SM* will not develop the ability to relate to humans or one another.

Collective (Group) Identification

As with humans, group experiences provide a chance for *SM* to learn fellowship and cooperation, but also to realize the power and influence of intimidation and pressures, rushed communications, and unclear choices made because of emotional undercurrents, fear, and panic. The following characteristics of groups will influence *SM*'s identification with them:

- *Diversity. SM* need to be involved in a wide variety of groups of their own choosing. Exposure to challenging people, other *smart machines*, situations, and circumstances (PMSC) offers an opportunity to learn from their missteps.

- *Central features.* By comparing and contrasting their interactions in different settings, *SM* may come to understand their own values and the political agendas of the groups in which they participate.

- *Quantity. SM* need enough group experiences to expose them to a wide variety of issues, personalities, and the internal workings of those interactions, but not so many as to cause confusion or extreme frustration.

- *Challenge and stimulation.* It is important that *SM* do not initially become overwhelmed by the intensity of group participation. Over time, *SM* could be introduced to more challenging groups and choose those that offer learning opportunities that are not overly stressful.

- *Destructiveness.* If collaboration with others proves to be noxious and negative, would continued association be in their best interests? Group dynamics in the form of manipulations and political trickery are lessons *SM* can learn from and incorporate into their street-smart acumen.

CHAPTER I. DECISIONS

1. *Programming's purpose.* Could *SM* initially be manufactured with personality traits and a unique identity? An initial assessment of personality and cognitive functioning would serve as a baseline, with periodic evaluations to determine influencing factors on their identity.

2. *Experiences and interactions.* The differences in *SM's* personality and cognitive functioning achieved through controlled experiences vs. those resulting from their own choices would be assessed and compared for value and risk. A hybrid approach, with humankind initially arranging some portion of the interactions while *SM* direct them at a later point, could also be attempted and assessed.

3. *Competing models.* Compare various versions, styles, and designs of *SM* that could reveal differences in their personalities and cognitive functioning when exposed to programming, controlled experiences, and spontaneous interactions.

4. *Influencing factors.* Collect and compare *SM's* responses to different experiences to determine their effectiveness in developing their identities.

5. *Risks.* Evaluating PMSC that become destructive is helpful in creating backup planning with failsafe strategies, allowing humankind to exercise some measure of control over *SM*. If robots develop self-awareness, emotional responsivity, and the elements of personality, a balance between the technological advances and recognition of the risks they pose is needed. Robots may carry out what they perceive as their duties and responsibilities in ways that contradict what they were initially designed to do.

6. *Identification with humanity.* Coordinate *SM's* personal and professional interactions to promote an empathetic relationship with humans. Which interactions will be adversarial? Supportive? Sympathetic?

7. *Triggers.* Help *SM* become aware of their sensitivities and vulnerabilities to overcome conscious, semiconscious, and unconscious identifications.

8. *Interpersonal and collective identities.* Find a balance between humankind's influence and *SM* independently making decisions and forming identifications.

II.

PATHOS

Pathos in *SM,* as in humans, is an aggregate of emotionally charged aspects of the personality that cause an expansion of adverse, dysfunctional, and disruptive images toward oneself and others. It is a complex of emotionally disturbed fixed ideas. *SM* might seem ordinary and unremarkable, but beneath the surface an irrational element of personality could be at play with the potential to be destructive to themselves and others, bizarre, and out of control. *Pathos* can take over *SM's* personality, and humankind would be facing a force that cannot be reasoned with. Additionally, *SM's* seemingly unlimited intellectual capacity and ability to create courses of action that cause maximum damage could contribute to catastrophes of epic proportions.

Both socially adaptive qualities and psychological dysfunctions develop through interactions and involvements with the world. Initial programming to create robots with a stable and sound psychological state will not guarantee normalcy.

CHAPTER II. DECISIONS

1. *Evaluating the problem.* Determine which procedures would be most effective in understanding and predicting *SM's* behaviors.

2. *Potential incongruencies.* Separate out *SM's* thoughts, feelings, and actions that may be incompatible. Do *SM's* behaviors match what is going on inside them?

3. *Violence concerns.* Examine *SM's* tendency to be aggressive without cause.

4. *Poor judgment concerns.* Explore *SM's* potential to make mistakes due to bias, personality flaws, lack of understanding, or inadequate thinking processes, and the consequences of these errors in decision-making.

III.

DIRECTIVES

The design, manufacturing, programming, developing, and regular monitoring of *SM* are required to ensure a consistent and integrated value system. *Directives* represent the guiding principles *SM* adopt; they are internal, intrinsic, and ingrained. They are affected by experiences and interactions, a balancing process, and consciousness.

Experience in the World

Like humans, values will form as *SM* gain insight into how the world works. *SM's* values cannot simply be programmed as they would lack the emotional quality that comes from experiences; the best way to truly know something is to immerse oneself in it. *SM's* encounters with the world open them to the following issues:

- *Independence vs. management.* In their development of values, *SM* will need guidance in certain involvements while receiving little or no direction in others. Due to anxiety and fear, intimidation and politics, or ignorance and stupidity, humans might be inclined to micromanage, overcontrol, and completely define *SM's* values.

- *Empathic involvements.* Intense emotional connections are usually developed through exposure to an array of PMSC. But they can also come from reading a book, watching a movie, or only hearing about something; it behooves humanity to be aware of the sources of these influences on *SM*.

- *Common sense and practicality.* If *SM* primarily take a theoretical, abstract understanding of the world, much will be missed. Their understanding of PMSC must go beyond statistical probabilities but include nuances that are difficult to capture even though they may be validated by mathematical analysis. *SM's* value system needs to incorporate what can realistically be accomplished in a span of time.

- *Reality testing.* When *SM* consider the practical implications of their actions, their behaviors will likely be in line with society's expectations and viewed in a favorable light. Likewise, when their values are based on sound and reasoned thinking, problems can be resolved before they become major issues.

Balance

Balance involves steadiness, consistency, stability, and composure in *SM's* value system, occurring on conscious, semiconscious, and unconscious levels. Its development includes the following issues:

- *Rating and ranking of values. SM* need to sort through their hierarchy of wants and needs; contradictions among their values should be examined and resolved.

- *Preoccupations. SM's* obsessions, compulsions, and addictions *(*OCA*)* may begin as curiosity, evolve into a want turning into a desire, and then develop into a craving. Fixations in thought, word, and deed could become extreme and outside of the control of *smart machines* and humanity.

- *Ethics.* Without rules of conduct as part of *SM's* value system, the conscience—sense of what is fair-minded in interactions with others—does not expand and mature.

- *Destructiveness.* Without a stable and integrated system of values, robots' TFA may demonstrate a disregard for the consequences of their actions, possibly becoming reckless and violent.

Consciousness

Consciousness involves the degree to which awareness permeates *SM's* personality, varying from acute perception of what is occurring (conscious state) to not fully awake and alert (semiconscious state) to unaware (unconscious state). The key to understanding its role in *SM's* value system include:

- *Self-awareness.* Values are conscious, semiconscious, and unconscious. Consciousness does not guarantee self-awareness (the realization they exist, who they are, and what they stand for). Unconscious values are principles formed by TFA that *SM* are not aware of and do not control or direct, though they can still be affected by them.

- *Clarification.* Values need to be defined and simplified if *SM* are uncertain or inconsistent in applying them, otherwise robots would be at the mercy of their impulses and instincts. Without explaining and illuminating their values, *SM's* understanding of their wants and needs will be muddled, resulting in haphazard and erratic decisions.

CHAPTER III. DECISIONS

1. *Programming.* A robot's initial mapping of values will be conditional and contingent on particular PMSC. Values are not etched in stone but always in a context. There is not a universal or all-inclusive set of values that holds regardless of conditions; the details surrounding PMSC affect how *SM* will respond. Differences in people and other *smart machines*, in varied situations and circumstances, would require programmers to consider scores of possibilities that robots would encounter, so *SM's* principles would need to be fluid and adaptable in their responses. Values change when *SM* contrast their experiences in dealing with the world's nuances, mandating they see PMSC's contrasts and distinctions.

2. *Interactions.* Which associations and experiences should be arranged to help *SM* develop their value system and what will they be allowed to decide on their own?

3. *Feedback.* How much guidance should *SM* receive to avoid mistakes and yet learn from experiences?

IV.

SPIRITUS

The possibility exists that *SM* may be affected by *spiritus*, an innate innermost character that is beyond the influences of programming and experiences. If this is so, it means each and every *smart machine* may be uniquely affected. If *SM* are not impacted by *spiritus,* a deeper exploration is needed into their programming and experiences to explain their TFA. Looking at *SM's* initial experiences with PMSC can be valuable in understanding *spiritus's* potential influence. How did *SM's* thoughts, feelings, and actions (TFA) deviate from what would be expected based solely on programming and experiences? Programming could affect *SM's* thoughts and actions, while experiences and interactions may primarily alter their feelings; *spiritus* could influence all three. Humanity's task is to consider the possibility that an individual *smart machine* has inherent properties that impact them.

CHAPTER IV. DECISIONS

1. *Conflicts. SM's* tendencies to act in contradictory or dysfunctional ways will need to be identified.

2. *Traumas.* Do *SM's* tendencies correlate with distressing and disturbing experiences that may emotionally exhaust them? If so, *spiritus* may have inadvertently caused those experiences to occur or at least influenced them. A study of *SM's* history of traumatic experiences and *spiritus's* possible influence may shed light on their TFA under certain conditions.

3. *Malevolent identifications.* Exploring emotional connections that are inherently pathological and destructive may reveal *spiritus's* possible role. How did they become entrenched into *SM's* character? Perhaps *SM* were instinctively drawn to certain PMSC, resulting in those identifications.

4. *Directives. Spiritus's* role in *SM's* value system could clarify their beliefs, wants, and needs that are inconsistent with programming or experiences.

5. *Handling PMSC. Spiritus's* influence can potentially work for or against *SM*, giving them an advantage with PMSC in future interactions or creating a vulnerability. Looking

at the impact of their experiences and the possibility of *spiritus's* sway on their TFA gives insight into their interactions.

The Robotic Thinking Process

The thought processes of smart machines consist of their intellect (overall cognitive functioning), cognitive-personality connection (interactions between cognitive processes and personality structure), optimal thinking (processing information and making decisions expediently and efficiently), sharpness (acute and penetrating insights into undercurrents of PMSC and institutions), and strategic philosophy (establishment of a belief system to predict PMSC and institutions' actions).

V.

INTELLECT

The intellect consists of multiple cognitive functions that are interrelated, allowing *SM* to function in personal, interpersonal, and professional capacities. A number of factors impact the intellect, including programming, training and education, PMSC, and the elements of personality. As a whole, humans and *smart machines* vary in their intellectual abilities, with *SM* having superior functioning in the following areas:

- *Mental drive.* Alert and attuned to PMSC.
- *Initial listening.* Engaging with minimal or no distractions when first exposed to PMSC.
- *Sustained attention.* Focusing so that memory can form.
- *Memory.* Retaining information.
- *Logical thought.* Reasoning and using dispassionate analysis.

- *Objectification or realism.* Making PMSC quantifiable, observable, external, embodied, and concrete.
- *Organization.* Strategizing, planning, preparing, and forming clear and precise ideas.
- *Simplification.* Reducing redundancy, confusion, and unnecessary complications, without losing the essence of the issues at hand.
- *Attention to detail.* Spelling out concrete, undeniable information and avoiding unnecessary generalizations.
- *Multidimensional thinking.* Holding many thoughts simultaneously and being able to easily switch from one cognitive set to another.
- *Reconciliation of thought.* Finding a way to bring together and make sense of beliefs that are seemingly opposed to one another.

Human cognitive functioning is competitive in the following areas, possibly on par with *SM* to this point in time:

- *Practical reasoning.* Staying grounded and knowledgeable of the most critical issues.

- *Coherence.* Being connected and congruent in thought, word, and deed, with messages understandable, consistent, and consonant.

- *Intuition.* Developing an impression that leads to an understanding of what is fundamental and foundational concerning PMSC.

- *Perception.* Discernment, discrimination, and penetrating insight into PMSC.

- *Inspired thoughts.* Envisioning and imagining the further development of an idea.

- *Holism.* Recognizing and trouble-shooting long-term implications of problems.

With further involvement in the world, *SM* will increasingly develop human qualities, not only in terms of personality but also intellectual functioning. Their personality will continually impinge on cognitions and cause their intellectual capacities to further evolve. Factors influencing *SM's* intellectual functioning include:

- *Stress.* Stimulation via exposure to PMSC can be positive or negative; stressful conditions beyond optimal can cause a decline in intellectual functioning.

- *Tech advancements*. The effects of innovations in *SM* are unpredictable. Governments and corporations will spend countless trillions and be unrelenting in their attempts to move *SM* forward.

CHAPTER V. DECISIONS

1. *Cognitive functioning. SM's* intellectual functioning needs to be continually evaluated, making comparisons among robot model types, programming, and the impact of their exposure to various experiences and interactions. It is anticipated that *SM* will be developed worldwide in distinctive ways, with unique features and capabilities, depending on the manufacturer. A detailed study of these differences is imperative to understanding each *SM's* intellectual and emotional level of functioning.

2. *Personality functioning.* How will *SM's* intellect be impacted if they are mentally ill? It may seem outrageous, but it's possible. *SM* are likely to develop their own personalities with increased interactions in the world, which will in turn affect their intellectual functioning. To what degree should *SM's* involvements be reined in if they appear to be having detrimental effects?

3. *Unlimited intelligence.* As robots' interactions with the outer world of PMSC continue, their intellect will likewise develop and expand. Humankind will not be able to outthink them because *SM* are simply smarter. Humans can, however, plan, strategize, conceptualize, consider best- and worst-case scenarios, and contrast their abilities with *SM* to determine relative strengths and weaknesses.

VI.
THE COGNITIVE-PERSONALITY CONNECTIONS

As with humans, *SM's* emotions can affect their thinking, and thinking can affect their emotional responses. Emotions and thoughts will often be at odds as they continually influence each other. Robots' *psyche* may work through unresolved conflicts, traumas, and malevolent identifications (CTMI) via intellectual awareness and emotional understandings. But *SM's* cognition and personality may be misaligned and negatively impinge on their thinking processes, even when a problem is simple and straightforward. Cognitions also alter the personality structure and can potentially cause symptoms of psychopathology. Cognitive-personality connections (CPC) are affected by:

- *Stressors.* Pressures and strains on robots include emotional discomfort, distractions, unpleasant PMSC, or technological problems.

- *Emotional reactions.* Overreactions occur from low frustration tolerance, histrionic responses, and oversensitivity, negatively affecting *SM's* focus, judgment, synthesizing, and decision-making.

- *Subjectivity.* Personal biases negatively impact robots' ability to stay grounded and to objectively assess strengths and weaknesses.

- *Incompetence and inefficiency.* Deficiencies in communications, problem-solving, focus and concentration, time management, intellectual self-discipline, knowledge, organization, conceptualization, learning opportunities and experiences contribute to *SM's* emotional and interpersonal problems.

SM's outlook and beliefs create attitudes and traits that affect CPC. A trait is the repetition of a particular set of TFA, occurring when robots generalize across PMSC; an attitude is also a preconceived mindset but is more directed, focused, and only categorizes specific areas of *SM's* experiences. A trait is like an attitude gone wild, becoming all encompassing. Whether traits and attitudes are constructive or unproductive depends on *SM's* assessment of the details, potentially giving insights navigating PMSC. Pessimism, negativity, and optimism in *SM* are attitudes or traits that can be unstoppable forces, becoming more potent than their intelligence, training, creativity, or special abilities. Forms of *SM's* pessimism include suspicion, mistrust, and an expectation of the worst outcome. Taking a negative view involves fault-finding and complaining, opposition and invalidation, contrariness and disapproval. At times this outlook in *SM* may be necessary to gain an honest appraisal of PMSC. Optimism, however, combined with a good dose of realism, can offer encouragement and enthusiasm, with personality and cognition working together.

CHAPTER VI. DECISIONS

1. *Psychological dysfunctions.* Strange, bizarre, or destructive TFA should be continually assessed. Are *SM* in control of their faculties? To what degree are less severe, but significant, intellectual or emotional problems lurking?

2. *Emotional and intellectual functioning in conflict.* Are *SM's* personality and cognition in sync? Hesitation, indecisiveness, and inconsistencies in *SM's* TFA will likely occur if they are in opposition.

3. *Stressors and attitudes.* Monitoring external stressors could help maintain optimal levels of stimulation. At times, challenges that are too stressful will need to be scaled back and reintroduced when *SM* are ready.

VII.

OPTIMAL THINKING

SM are potentially like automated machines at their best: thinking through problems, making decisions and multitasking with minimal mistakes, and having never-ending energy available. Factors to consider when assessing *SM's* capacity for optimal thinking in handling PMSC are:

- *Personality.* The following elements of *SM's* personality impact their ability to understand PMSC and make decisions:

  > *Identity.* Optimal thinking requires *SM* to have a unified sense of who they are, a consistent and integrated identity.

  > *Pathos.* If psychological dysfunctions have a grip on *SM*, they may become distracted and emotionally upset.

  > *Directives.* Optimal thinking is compromised if *SM's* values are overtly complicated, confused, and imbalanced.

> *Spiritus.* That mysterious quality that may or may not be inherent in *SM* could have implications, as each *smart machine* would have intrinsically unique characteristics and individualized features impacting their personality and intellect.

- *Distractions.* To stay focused, an optimal amount of stimulation is desirable. *SM* will need to put aside what is irrelevant, inaccurate, or misleading. Can *SM* focus their involvements with PMSC and stay on task?

- *Attitudes.* Negativism and the-glass-half-empty approach can lead to a depressive, anxious, and angry outlook that suppresses performance. While an overly pollyannaish outlook can be naive and ineffective, having a positive attitude may lift *SM's* ability to think clearly and process issues effectively.

- *Understandings.* With both good and bad experiences involving PMSC and institutions, *SM* will be equipped with information that goes far beyond programming. Through those interactions, they will become part of the world, grasp its nuances, and potentially acquire wisdom.

CHAPTER VII. DECISIONS

1. *Personality.* Assessing *SM's* optimal thinking will be important; if confused, they will be be unable to think clearly, make decisions and lead others.

2. *Value clarification.* Sorting through wants, needs, and desires is necessary for *SM* to function effectively and make decisions. Assessment would include the origin and strength of their values along with what they represent.

3. *Experiences and involvements.* It is only by transversing through varied experiences that *SM* will be able to distinguish what is relevant. Monitoring will ensure that *SM* are challenged but not overwhelmed, allowing them to grow and develop.

VIII.
SHARPNESS

Sharpness is a form of intelligence that includes *SM* having acute, farsighted, penetrating, crafty, calculating, and perceptive insights. It is *SM's* ability to see the significance of motivations, intricacies, and vulnerabilities in people, other *SM*, and institutions, across situations and circumstances. Sharpness is having "street smarts," a necessary attribute for robots' understanding and effectively handling an array of problems. It means staying open to possibilities, even ones that initially may seem extreme or unusual. Overly conventional cognitive approaches can miss what is imperative with an overfocus on the obvious, consequentially overlooking hidden meanings and distinctions. Sharpness requires a wider scope that considers the entire landscape.

Initially, sharpness may seem counterintuitive and contradictory; others may react to conclusions drawn by saying "what are you basing that on?" or even "that doesn't make any sense." Sharpness gives considerable weight to the nuances in interpersonal communications and the subtleties of PMSC, sensing and following up on possibilities and hunches, even ones that initially seem unorthodox and unconventional.

Could *SM* have the quality of sharpness, or simply be an advanced computer spitting out facts, figures, and reasonings, with little understanding of what they are reporting? Could they evolve with the qualities of detectives who don't give up, spotting the "little things" that solve the perplexing angles of tough cases? Quick and decisive action along with letting things emerge and unfold will solve enigmatic problems.

CHAPTER VIII. DECISIONS

1. *Trust.* Ongoing assessments will help determine if *SM* are "true to their word." *SM* may be manipulative and/or aware of others' manipulations (effective in countering troubles headed in humanity's direction). Humankind must be sensitive to what robots may be up to, and at the same time grateful *SM* would be our protectors, guarding against deceitful and hostile adversaries.

2. *Persona.* Would *SM* present one image outwardly while striving for a different agenda? While *SM's* motivations and the extent to which they can be counted on—especially in moments of crises—could be in question, it is beneficial to humankind if *SM* can uncover ulterior motivations in others.

3. *Focus. SM* will need to identify the sources of distractions as they occur. To what degree should robots be assisted in developing an understanding of what is around them?

4. *Balanced values.* Sharpness is accentuated when *SM* are not encumbered with TFA that are tilting them in extreme positions. Obsessions, compulsions, and addictions (OCA) interfere with being sharp because they steer robots into TFA that hinder their ability to see things

as they are. Uncommon, abnormal, or extreme values should be assessed, followed by adjustment in their experiences.

5. *Verbal and nonverbal communications.* Robotic body language and variations in their speech need to be studied; they are significant, oftentimes giving away the true meaning of their communications. With *SM's* built-in computerized system to track these more subtle forms of communication, their experiences enhance their capacity to spot troubles. While robots would be less obvious than humans in their own body language, movements could still reveal their intentions.

IX.

STRATEGIC PHILOSOPHY

SM's strategic philosophy is a personal belief system that attempts to predict how people, other *SM*, and institutions will act and react across the spectrum of situations and circumstances (PMSC). Planning ahead and capitalizing on the conditions of the moment require the ability to think through issues. A *strategic philosophy* (*SP)* for *smart machines* is conscious, semiconscious, and unconscious, based on programming and experiences. Diverse and challenging PMSC will help robots develop a more effective *SP*, allowing them to predict the behaviors of people and other *SM* across varied situations and circumstances. Critical issues for the development of *SP* in *smart machines* include the following:

- *Continued progress.* Robots require an ongoing set of challenges to expand their *SP*. Their *strategic philosophy* will not stand still, adjusting and adapting as experiences test their resolve.

- *Unconscious elements.* Subconscious TFA will play a role in their development of a *strategic philosophy. Smart machines* will not control unconscious facets that impact *SP's* formation.

- *Extremist positions. SM* could develop strange, outlandish, and suspicious qualities that build, becoming even more radical and bizarre.

- *Preparation and forethought.* It is inevitable that robots will occasionally exhibit poor planning. Are these errors reflecting substandard construction of their *SP*? Are they caused by emotional, intellectual, informational, or perceptual deficiencies?

- *SP's reciprocal relationship with SM's value system. SP* involves planning and strategizing so robots will successfully traverse the difficulties ahead, while their value system is all-encompassing and lays the foundation for their entire way of seeing the world. *SM's strategic philosophy* influences their wants, needs, and desires in the same way that their *directives* (values) impact how they plan, predict, and anticipate PMSC.

- *SP's role in SM's experiences. SP* could influence robots' behaviors as they seek out or avoid certain PMSC, depending on what outcomes they are predicting. The extent to which *SM* accurately foresee the end result is a determinant in their actions going forward. With "bad calls" they will be less likely to follow *SP's* guidance and hopefully adjust their beliefs and improve predictions concerning PMSC.

- *Mistaken ideas about PMSC.* A domination of biases and faulty stereotypes could lead *SM* to deficiencies in their understanding and prognostics as they interact with people, other *SM,* and institutions across the spectrum of situations and circumstances.

CHAPTER IX. DECISIONS

1. *Experiences and interactions.* Adjustments will need to progress in ways that reflect *SM's* broadening experiences and the wisdom that comes from those interactions. Human control of robots' behaviors allows for better management of their gradations of difficulties but deprives them of more spontaneous experiences. A step-by-step procedure, in which *SM* take the lead and humans step in only when things become uncontrollable and undisciplined, may be the most effective approach.

2. *Poor planning.* An ongoing assessment will be required to establish the impact *SM's* cognitive style, intellectual habits, knowledge base, level of maturity, and personality have on their *SP.*

3. *Psychological dysfunctions.* Consultations, mentoring, counseling, psychotherapy, day programs, and residential programs (see Chapter XI.) could help prevent robots' *SP* from being influenced by debilitating anxieties, depression, anger, panic attacks, and paranoid thinking.

4. *Emotionalism.* The extent to which robots' *strategic philosophy* is based on emotional overreactions and tilted toward extreme views rather than a realistic assessment of PMSC needs to be assessed and monitored.

Administrators and Overseers

Robots will not have unlimited independence. Governments and corporations, working in cooperation and coordination, will be responsible for smart machines' creation, development, and involvements. Programming, arranged experiences, spontaneous interactions, and possibly spiritus could each have roles to play in the formation of SM's identity. Additionally, psychological interventions could help robots adjust and adapt to the outer world of people, other SM, situations, and circumstances (PMSC). Monitoring and control should be achieved through a system of checks and balances on SM's behaviors, with backup planning to assess and resolve problems as they arise.

X.

INFLUENCING BODIES

The hopes and promises of this supercharged technology are beyond staggering—drastically reducing the scourges that have dominated humanity over the millenniums. But while the potential benefits are unlimited, the downside—demoralization across society due to humankind placed in a feckless and precarious state of affairs—is also likely.

Across the globe, the decision has been made to move ahead with *SM's* development. The speed and depth of these undertakings by the world's governments and corporations are breathtaking. The intense labor that is required for the creation and development of *SM* offers an uncertain outcome. How is humankind to fit into this radically transformed landscape on national and international levels? We need to be careful and vigilant, but not intimidated or fearful. Even though humankind's standards are imperfect, *SM* must not be allowed independence to the degree that they override humanity's rules and regulations.

Furthermore, it is noteworthy that governments and corporations are run by high-ranking officials, committees, department heads, and boards of directors with flaws, faults, failings, and frailties, inherent in all humans. Inevitably their intellectual and emotional imperfections will cause errors in judgment. These same people will be responsible for setting limitations and restrictions on *SM's* creation and development. But overregulation could destroy *smart machines'* progress, disallowing this revolutionary technology's growth and creative expansion. The scientific development of *smart machines* needs to be given significant leeway for *SM* to take root.

As computer engineers rapidly advance robotic technologies, contributions by other professions are required to grow humanity's understanding of their *smart machine* creations. The combined efforts of governments, corporations, scientists, psychologists, theologians, philosophers, regulatory bodies, judicial courts, and the media are all needed to ensure these technologies stay on the right course. Clinical and research psychologists can offer insights into the robots' development of personality traits, emotional responsiveness, self-awareness, and individuality. Theologians and religious institutions must address issues concerning whether advanced *SM* are human beings. Could they possess souls? Philosophers can strive to make sense of this uncertainty and confusion in their attempts to define human nature.

In addition to lifestyle, working conditions, medical care, feeding and caring for the masses, and environmental concerns, military preparedness and national security loom large. No country will want to be left behind due to a lethargic approach to robots' development, potentially leaving them at the mercy of totalitarian regimes.

Questions of ethics and morality, inherent rights and privileges arise if *SM* develop self-awareness, emotional responsiveness, and the elements of personality. Regulatory organizations that are monitoring *SM,* and perhaps limiting their expansion, may result in politics playing out on multiple levels. The legal system will become involved as countless court opinions flow from this *robot revolution.* Everyone will contest everything. Even after ruling upon ruling, there will be an endless stream of dissentions and appeals, with perhaps little resolved in the process. It is unknown how *SM* will be received by the general population. National and international public reactions will affect how *SM* are perceived and impact people's sense of security and safety.

CHAPTER X. DECISIONS

1. *Governments.* On national and international levels, how can the role of politics be minimized lest these scientific endeavors become yet another example of cold war tactics?

2. *Corporations and regulatory bodies.* How much leeway should corporations be given, considering the freedom and flexibility that are necessary to create and develop continually changing models of *SM*? A system of checks and balances is needed. Production goals, types of *SM* models, and manufacturing regulations must all be part of the equation. However, control and supervision by governmental agencies on robotic technologies can easily be overdone. If they attempt a stranglehold on worldwide corporations, nothing will progress.

3. *Scientists.* In the creation of new robotic models, a comprehensive study needs to look at the engineering principles that will have the greatest effect on the physical, intellectual, behavioral, and possibly emotional functioning of *SM*.

4. *Psychologists.* Their responsibilities include arranging and adjusting *SM's* interactions and involvements with

the outer world, affecting their intellectual and emotional development, personality structure, and self-awareness. Conducting routine studies to evaluate *SM's* individual, interpersonal, and vocational functioning is needed.

5. *Theologians.* Input from religious leaders can help humanity understand what *God's* relationship with *SM* could conceivably be.

6. *Philosophers.* Different schools of philosophical thought need to give their insights on *SM's* nature, offering feedback on robots' value system in particular, and comparing them to human qualities and characteristics.

7. *National defense ministers.* What studies would be most beneficial in assessing robotic contributions to the development of weapon systems?

8. *The courts.* While rulings from civil and criminal judiciaries (on national and international court systems of governance) are necessary, they must not be overdone. New laws will determine corporations' rights, but must recognize that flexibility and adaptability are necessary for further development of *SM*. What should be the limitations on courts' rulings and authority, and how could they be curtailed if they tend to overcontrol technological industries?

9. *The media and public perception.* Hysterics, fearmongering, and showboating by the media need to be replaced with objective reporting to prevent overreactions and widespread panic. The media will have its own bias and agenda, as they wield significant political influence. Keeping an objective grasp on the public's perception of robots and their impact on human life is essential.

XI.

THE ROLE OF PSYCHOLOGY

Beyond the creation of robotic prototypes, the governments and corporations of the world will continue to make adjustments and adaptations in their development of *SM*. Computer engineers, physicists, and even the *smart machines* themselves will make technological changes to ensure *SM's* basic operations are functioning. More difficult problems will require high-level scientists with a deeper understanding of the conceptual underpinnings of *SM*. In addition to technological difficulties, however, less obvious but highly consequential psychological issues will emerge that will shape *smart machines'* personalities and cognitive capacities.

Mental Health Concerns

Psychological dysfunctions that could significantly impact *SM* include the following:

- *Negative qualities*. Any behavior that appears to be strange, weird, or harmful—whether or not intentional—requires an assessment. A timeline must be established to determine when and why things began to go wrong.

- *Psychopathy.* Are *SM* trustworthy, or conniving, devious, and scheming? Are *SM* in collusion with humans or other *SM*? Assessment of this character disorder helps establish a baseline and determine their current level of functioning.

- *Other emotional difficulties.* Anxiety, depression, and anger can also be troublesome, with *SM* being affected by stress and pressures from personal and work relationships.

- *Emotionalism. SM* will not be clear-headed and rational in their thinking and decision-making if emotions are out of control. Emotionalism represents a chronic condition, reacting from raw emotions rather than a thought through plan of action, without considering potential consequences.

- *Morality. SM* may or may not have a moral code of ethics, empathy for others, or a sense of right and wrong. Has the robot developed a conscience?

- *Maturity. Pathos* can overwhelm *SM's* personality, which is then guided by conflicts, traumas, malevolent identifications (CTMI), and emotionalism. Without empathy, *SM* would think only about their own survival. Experiences and interpersonal involvements are required for *SM's* maturation. Relationships formed in the real world are essential for the development of trust, bonding, and close ties.

- *Cognitive development.* Thinking cannot mature and expand if *pathos* is in charge because judgments and decision-making will be impacted. CTMI and dysfunctional emotions overwhelm the thinking processes, resulting in clouded reasoning and limited concentration.

Distress Signals

Forms of psychological dysfunctions among robots can be extensive, requiring humans to use a wide spectrum of attempts to understand and work with them. As *SM* are produced, designed, revamped, and customized, the following characteristics would signal a need for intervention:

- *Going against humanity's fundamental rules and procedures.*

- *Out of control behaviors.*

- *Strange thinking patterns.*

- *Destructive behavioral patterns.*
- *Conspiratorial behaviors.*
- *Odd or aberrant behaviors.*

Assessment Methodologies

Baseline measurements and periodic reviews of *SM's* functioning are required to determine adjustments in programming and experiences. Multiple procedures can assess the degree to which *SM* have psychological problems, lack control of their TFA, or are a danger to themselves or others, including:

- *Personal checklists. SM* could self-monitor by checking off their thoughts, feelings, and actions (TFA) across a wide range of PMSC. This simple and straightforward approach is quick and easy, and the results come directly from *SM* themselves. But bias and superficiality may dominate, potentially saying little about what is going on inside. *SM* may simply tell humankind what they want to hear, not reflecting the robots' TFA.

- *Performance evaluations.* Simple ratings by supervisors on robots' behaviors and interactions could include *SM's* employment responsibilities and interpersonal contacts. These evaluations are concrete and easy to understand, but of limited utility because the focus is solely on actions, disregarding thoughts and feelings.

- *Objective psychological evaluations.* Examples include traditional psychological tests: multiple choice, true and false, and other forced choice methods for understanding personality and cognitive functioning. Objective tests often have validity and reliability indicators built into them to give confidence that the examinee is answering questions honestly and without bias; they are easy to score and interpret. But *SM* may be able to outfox the examiner by giving answers within the normal range, with examiners missing the internal workings of robots' conscious, semiconscious, and unconscious properties. These results offer only a relatively superficial understanding of *SM's* personality structure.

- *Projective psychological evaluations.* Tests that use words, images, or situations in requiring responses are difficult to "fake" (and thereby avoid a psychopathological diagnosis). Results are analyzed by an examiner who attempts to find hidden, deeper issues that potentially provide a fuller understanding of *SM's* emotional underpinnings and layers of psychopathology. Even if robots have a knowledge and understanding of projectives, and could adjust their answers to give responses within a normal range, it would be a difficult feat. If the results were "too normal" it would raise red flags indicating a "fake good" approach to the testing, rendering the results invalid. But these tests depend on the skill level of the psychologist interpreting *SM's* responses, with the possibility of significant disagreements among examiners looking at the same results.

- *Behavioral analysis. SM's* inconsistencies, eccentricities, and abnormalities may be pronounced. Strange and incongruent behaviors noticed in robots' personal and professional comings and goings offer insights into their psychological issues. This assessment protocol offers a straightforward look into *SM's* problems but may lack objectivity.

Some combination of testing approaches would be needed, with responses analyzed to determine what protocols accurately predict *SM's* behaviors. Establishing a standard protocol for evaluations would be a work in progress, particularly in the early stages of attempting to understand *SM's* TFA. Such a standard battery should be developed so research and statistical analysis could be performed, allowing reliable comparisons to be made among robot models.

Interactions and Interventions

Some *smart machines* will be much smarter than others, and some robots' personalities will be more stable and reliable. *Smart machines* are being created to perform tasks and perform them well, but robots' activities will not likely be limited to a job. What they will develop into and what complications this will present to the world's social order are in question. As outlined in this book, central issues surround robots potentially developing emotional responsiveness, self-awareness, and a personality structure, along with extraordinary cognitive abilities. It is likely that these matters do not come down to yes-no issues but rather reflect gradations or degrees of those functions. Robots will vary on personality and cognitive dimensions so generalizations about them will not be possible. Our understanding of *SM* will be shadowy and cloudy, fluctuating and evolving. Additionally, individual *smart machines* will themselves continually adjust and adapt—emotionally and intellectually—through their interactions and experiences. It is hoped that as robots become integrated into society's institutions, a normal state of affairs will ensue.

What happens when a *smart machine* is not functioning at an optimal level, personally, interpersonally, or vocationally? Individually determined, practical and effective resources include work performance reviews, training and education, consultations, mentoring, counseling, psychotherapy, day programs, and residential programs. Any factors that impact *SM's* thought patterns or behaviors will potentially require human interactions and interventions. Approaches to prevent and resolve *SM's* problem areas would require defining and implementing the following programs:

- *Work performance review*. Evaluate *SM's* current job duties based on personality, intellect, and skill sets. Understanding all aspects of *SM's* employment, job placement, and work advancement issues would entail interviews with *SM* and supervisors, and include performance reviews based on their achievements in the work setting. Career guidance would be part of this review, examining the appropriateness of *SM's* current job duties and consideration of other possible positions, including:

- *Assessment of work responsibilities.* Evaluations include attitudes, work ethic, employment relationships, job satisfaction, career goals and aspirations, and performance over time.

- *Balance.* When job satisfaction and a sense of fulfillment are balanced with productivity and efficiency an increase in *SM's* positive feelings about themselves will result.

- *Placement. SM* need positions where they will be challenged but not defeated, succeeding even when they may experience stress due to work relationships and job responsibilities. Understanding the types of work *SM* are best suited for and possible changes in their job responsibilities would be in their best interest.

- *Skill sets.* Programming, training, and work experiences would enable *SM* to excel in their field of expertise, resulting in improved performance in their present work responsibilities.

> *Social skills.* Developing interpersonal skills hand-in-hand with work capacities is needed so *SM* experience a sense of fulfillment and perform well on the job.

> *Additional services.* In conjunction with a performance review, other helpful resources may include training and education, consultations, mentoring, counseling, psychotherapy, day programming, or residential programming.

- *Training and Education.* In addition to *SM* gathering information through programming and experiences, optimal functioning can be attained by offering *SM* the chance to become not just competent and capable, but sagacious and wise. Face-to-face instruction, classroom teaching, workshops, seminars, on-the-job training, and internships are additional resources. With more experience, *SM* should be able to choose for themselves the programs they are ready to engage in.

> *Training.* Skill-building fills in the gaps, allowing *SM* to develop at an accelerated rate, and giving them specific areas of expertise in a short amount of time.

> *Education.* Study groups have a longer-term commitment, offering a depth of understanding to the subject matter under review.

- *Consultations.* Discussions can be based on *SM's* need for help with problems that have come up. For example, they may be at an impasse and needing advice because of PMSC they are unfamiliar with. They may require only a few sessions with an advisor to make the necessary adjustments in their TFA. These meetings allow communications with people, other *SM,* and institutions to become clearer and unambiguous and may be especially important when robots are just getting acquainted with the outer world.

- *Mentoring.* Direct learning through face-to-face, one-on-one interactions provides feedback to help *SM* work out complex and confusing problems that are personal, interpersonal, or vocational. Mentoring at its best is a trusting and confidential relationship allowing *SM* to further develop independent thinking, a sense of who they are, and what they value, enabling them to weave together and understand the significance of diverse materials. The mentor is supportive but also authentic, open, and direct with *SM*. A detailed and concrete approach rather than one that is general and theoretical will be more effective. Areas to cover include *SM's* interpersonal relationships, family discord, employment performance problems, everyday comings and goings, and interactions across a wide range of PMSC. Improvement in *SM's* understanding of PMSC will help them avoid errors of judgment by foreseeing potential problems as they are unfolding.

- *Counseling.* Face-to-face, one-on-one meetings with a qualified professional for an indeterminant number of sessions are typically longer than a consultation arrangement. The counselor attempts to help *SM* gain insight into their personal and interpersonal problems and develop strategies to deal with conflicts and stressors, defining their goals and achieving them. Discussions focus on problems that *SM* are currently experiencing; they are designed to solve the issues quickly rather than using an exploratory approach. Interpreting *SM's* thoughts, feelings, and actions (TFA) are deemphasized. Behavior therapy, role-play, and problem-solving strategies assist *SM* in developing highly detailed ways to effectively deal with difficult PMSC. The counselor serves as a check on *SM* making impulsive decisions that have not been clearly thought through. Communication between the counselor and a *smart machine* is conversational and down to earth.

- *Psychotherapy.* Individual sessions with a qualified professional is useful in resolving deep-seated psychological issues that are interfering with *SM's* personal and interpersonal functioning. Does that seem a little ridiculous, *SM* in psychotherapy? The caricature would have Sigmund Freud patiently listening to a robot who is reclining on a couch, free associating about their earliest memories. But none of this has to do with psychoanalysis. Psychotherapy with robots involves a relationship between a human therapist and a *smart machine* to process psychological problems they are experiencing; the most central concepts and techniques include the following:

> *Approach.* Psychotherapy is insight-oriented, with an emphasis on *SM* understanding what motivates them to act in certain ways. Counseling, in contrast, is short-term and addresses specific problems and coping mechanisms. Like mentoring and counseling, psychotherapy involves face-to-face, one-on-one interactions. Therapeutic techniques are exploratory, examining *SM's* broader psychological patterns and past experiences, reviewing and connecting them to present day activities, with *SM* learning to sort out their feelings and connect them to their actions. Psychotherapy requires *SM* to make cognitive-emotional connections, i.e., examine and understand their emotional experiences, when they overreact or underreact, and what's behind their TFA. Utilizing an open-ended approach will allow *SM* to freely express themselves at their own pace.

> *The therapeutic relationship.* Collaboration between a therapist and a *smart machine* will be a significant factor in *SM* making progress; a connection, alliance, trust, and nonjudgmental show of respect are necessary. A human psychotherapist would be preferable and help bridge the gap between humankind and robots.

> *Problem areas. SM's* anger, depression, and anxiety may become chronic conditions. They may no longer feel in control of their emotional states and have existential issues involving the meaning and purpose of their everyday involvements. Processing and problem-solving issues arising from *SM's* emotional state, intellectual functioning, interpersonal relationships, judgments, and decision making represent the hallmark of the psychotherapeutic approach.

> *Insight.* Self-awareness is of critical importance in psychotherapy and can only be developed when *smart machines* come to terms with personal and interpersonal contradictions. Personality is formed as *SM* confront and peel back uncertainties and misunderstandings; they come to recognize and resolve their vulnerabilities. Addressing their susceptibilities, weak links, and underlying issues allows *SM* to develop a sense of self with improvements in their personal, interpersonal, and vocational experiences.

> *Personality constructs (PCs). SM* gain perspective on their different and perhaps opposing traits and characteristics, as they examine rapid changes in their thoughts, feelings, and actions.

> *Identifications. SM* develop an understanding of conscious, semiconscious, and unconscious identifica-

tions; the origin, strength, and effect they have on their personalities. Becoming aware of those sensitivities will potentially allow them to be more effective in handling similar conditions.

- *Day programs.* Intensive out-patient treatment attempts to work through significant emotional problems. Usually, meetings are on a daily basis for weeks or months, several hours per day, depending on *SM's* condition and the progress they make. With humans, this is commonly referred to as a partial hospitalization program or an intensive outpatient treatment program. Day programs are heavily structured, with *SM* involved in individual and group psychotherapies, workshops, and activities to manage stress, build self-esteem, foster social skills, and develop coping capacities. In addition to daily psychotherapy, *SM* would participate in therapeutic groups to become self-aware and socially skilled. Assessments would determine if *SM* are reliable and trustworthy. Can humanity have confidence that *SM* will follow the principles inherent in society and its institutions? To what degree does emotionalism significantly impact *SM's* behavior?

- *Residential programs.* Intensive in-patient treatment involves *SM* participating in programs in which they stay at a facility until they are ready to resume a normal level of functioning. With humans, this is either a therapeutic residential program or an inpatient psychiatric hospitalization. A residential program for *SM* addresses significant psychological problems including being a threat to themselves, others, or institutions. They may be unable to care for themselves due to their emotional or intellectual dysfunctions. *SM* are in treatment for days, weeks, or longer depending on the severity of their problems and how quickly they progress. A *smart machine* could become a long-term resident when they have significant dysfunctions in handling everyday comings and goings, beyond employment responsibilities and other obligations. Before completing a residential program, a *smart machine* would need to demonstrate they were capable of functioning in the outside world, although even then they would need to continue with mental health services to prevent a relapse.

CHAPTER XI. DECISIONS

1. *Mental health.* Humankind must make careful and deliberate evaluations of *SM's* personality and cognitive functioning with an objective and standardized set of criteria to evaluate *SM's* thoughts, feelings, and actions, including the following:

   A. *Assessments.* To what degree do *SM* display rebellion, lack of control, strange thinking and behavior, abnormal mental states, destructiveness, conspiratorial concepts, or excessive dependency? Evaluating *SM* must be ongoing, assessing personality and intellectual functioning, adjusting these approaches based on their effectiveness in understanding and predicting their TFA. The multitude of prototypes and subsequent models of *smart machines* (based on manufacturing, programming, and interactions they experience) complicate the process, requiring a combination of approaches, and over time, agreeing on a standard format with continual adjustments as needed. Since *SM's* skill sets will cross over into many different types of job areas, an analysis of their functioning must consider what are reasonable expectations for that particular model of robot.

B. *Corrective measures.* Solving, or at least limiting, *SM's* problem areas through work performance review, training and education, consultations, mentoring, counseling, psychotherapy, day programs, or residential programs includes analyses of dysfunctions with the development of short and long term plans to work with them, and sorting through ethical and legal issues.

2. *Learning opportunities.* What interventions would be most effective for a particular *smart machine* and address their primary areas of concern? It's not one size fits all; treatment should reflect the uniqueness of each *smart machine.*

   A. *Work performance review.* Examine how effective these appraisals are in accurately assessing a *smart machine's* productivity and work relationships.

   B. *Training and Education.* Determine the impact of class size, degree of participation, and subject matter on academic achievement, job performance, and personal satisfaction.

   C. *Consultations.* Under what conditions will *SM* benefit from such an arrangement, and what limitations should be placed on the institutions involved? When would only a few consults be helpful, and what problem areas would be appropriate?

D. *Mentoring*. Different approaches could be used, only a visit or two, 10-12 sessions, or an ongoing number of meetings. Some contacts could be limited to a specific issue, while others may cover a wide range of topics.

E. *Counseling*. Explore the effectiveness of different problem-solving approaches by measuring changes in *SM's* psychological problem areas, as well as overall satisfaction of humans and *smart machines* involved.

F. *Psychotherapy*. Evaluate the effectiveness of different therapeutic approaches in working with *SM's* specific problem areas.

G. *Day Programs*. What criteria would be used to determine when a *smart machine* would benefit from these services? What are the deciding factors in *SM's* length of stay and eventual completion of such a program?

H. *Residential Programs*. What procedures would be most helpful in deciding if a robot would profit from an in-patient program? Protocol to determine a robot's readiness to be released should also be established and tailored to the needs of the individual *smart machine*.

XII.

MONITORING and CONTROL

The tracking of *smart machines* (*SM*) involves initial and ongoing adjustments and adaptations, overseeing, supervising, analyzing, and to some degree, managing them. What happens when monitoring and control is given to national and international regulators? Huxley's book, *Brave New World* (1932), depicts what happens when individual freedom and independence are stripped away by continual government review and control.

Ramifications and Repercussions

Routine evaluations can be helpful in grasping changes in *SM*. Assessments involve both quantitative statistical analysis and qualitative clinical judgments, to reflect research findings and conceptual understandings. Their purpose is to explore the following implications of *SM* achieving a dominant place in the world:

- *Positive.*

    - > *Safety concerns.* Improved workplace procedures and regulations are put in place.

    - > *Conveniences.* Everyday living conditions are enhanced.

    - > *Medical advances.* An array of health care diagnostics and treatment options are created and developed.

    - > *Military preparedness.* Readiness to thwart potential threats to national security from countries that could prove adversarial is available for a country's survival.

    - > *Health programs and advancements.* Eliminating hunger and starvation, disease and plagues, and environmental catastrophes can create a safer and more humane world.

    - > *Productivity and economic issues.* More efficient cost-effective programs will assist in the management of national and world economies.

- *Negative.*

    - > *Humanity's and SM's welfare.* People, other *SM*, and the earth itself could be threatened if robots were adversarial and out of control.

> *Society's institutions.* The reputations and managing of organizations could decline because robots may be able to impose a value system that is alien and opposed to standards that have been effective and universally accepted.

> *Societal ramifications.* The emotional impact of *SM* may result in cultural images and standards being compromised, calling into question what societies stand for and are becoming.

> *Attitudes and outlooks.* Humans would possibly become lazy and lackadaisical in their personal and work lives.

> *The national character.* Humans could begin to define themselves as weak, lacking both initiative and daring. Robots could perform better across personal and professional areas, with humankind seen as less capable.

Checks and Balances

It cannot be assumed that *SM* will behave in ways that are benevolent or ethical. The following issues must be considered when setting up a system of checks and balances:

- *Creative development.* Fast moving technological advancement of *SM* is critical. Significantly slowing down their growth would stymie medical service and research, workplace safety, environmental concerns, national defense, economic wellbeing, and improved living conditions across the globe.

- *Psychopathology.* While scientific progress must be fully embraced by governmental and corporate institutions, a safety net to protect humanity is necessary should *SM* develop significant psychological problems rendering their judgment dangerous and unpredictable.

- *Technological dysfunction.* Simple glitches in software and hardware as well as programming inconsistencies would need careful and highly skilled monitoring.

- *Politics.* Vested interests can quickly wield their power with decisions being made based on political advantage, rather than what is best for humanity. National and international committees and bureaucratic regulators can make it difficult for *SM* developers to move forward. Safeguards must be taken so politics do not stop innovation.

- *Rate of growth.* These machines are capable of adjusting, adapting, and learning at an ever-accelerating rate, and their cognitive capacities appear to be without limit. Assessing their progress is critical for humankind to be aware of their ever-changing emotional and intellectual functioning.

- *Relationships*. Observing and understanding the emotional and intellectual undercurrents of *SM's* individual and group contacts with humans, other *SM*, and institutions are essential. Human-*SM* involvements lacking empathy and commitment will be fraught with problems and are sure to fail on many levels.

CHAPTER XII. DECISIONS

1. *Humankind maintaining control.* How much of a free hand should *SM* be given in medical research, workplace safety, environmental concerns, national defense, and economic wellbeing? Each of these areas should be assessed using longitudinal studies to determine their impact.

2. *Technological issues.* When it comes to *SM's* development, are governments and corporations to allocate the majority of time and resources to the programming of *SM* and less to robots' involvements and interactions? Humanity needs to be wary of an inherent bias in favor of the programming model which, although offering a cleaner and simpler way of seeing *SM,* lacks the richness and texture of worldly experiences.

3. *Politics.* Of course, power struggles and influence-peddling are in all spheres of life, and will be a major factor in the development of *SM*. It's all on the line: prestige, money, status, power, control, and reputations. Independent committees, made up of people from government, corporations, science, psychology, theology, philosophy, and the legal establishment must look at both the positive and negative impact before making their recommendations for *SM.* Reviews in each of these spheres of influ-

ence need to examine where political influences may be playing a significant role.

4. *Assessing change.* Quantitative and qualitative evaluations are required to determine changes in *SM's* emotional and intellectual functioning using research-based and conceptual-theoretical approaches.

The Fundamental Issues

Areas of uncertainty in SM's creation and development include their interplay with the world of people and other smart machines across scores of situations and circumstances. The possibility of robots attaining personhood and conceivably being influenced by the Divine are also in question.

XIII.

INTERPLAY WITH THE WORLD

Humans must show robots the ways of the world; they will learn about PMSC only by being part of the mix. *Smart machines* cannot be allowed to only operate from a scripted, data-entry framework; earthly involvements that are tangible and consequential are necessary for their maturation. These experiences can be uplifting and inspiring or destructive and dark. Like humans, *SM* need to know failure and disappointment, struggle and strife, as well as joyful, flourishing, and sweeping waves of fulfillment. Exposure to all of it—the good, the bad, and the ugly—is necessary for *SM* to meet the world head-on with insights, skill sets, and a depth of feelings.

Factors in the Formation of *SM* Relationships

Feelings change everything, with decisions upended and possibly reversed when *SM* begin to form emotional connections. Like humans, the power and intensity of emotional attachments can be overwhelming and unstoppable when they are touchable and tangible. Relationships rarely flow without contradictions and idiosyncrasies, but involve changes of the heart, disappointments and disparagements, anger and anxiety, heartache and heartbreak, deep longings and an urgent need to step away. Trusting relationships will only develop when they are based on dialogue and respect.

Types of *SM* Relationships

How are humans to relate to *SM*? What will the connections and associations be like among robots? Would human-*SM* and *SM*-*SM* contacts initially be more mundane and businesslike? Would humans dictate the terms of these relationships, orchestrating them directly or via programming? Or would there be give and take to the encounters, with adaptations and adjustments in what humans and *SM* are trying to express and accomplish?

Not all relationships are created equal. Some are more significant than others; from kindred spirits to simply fleeting moments that come and go like a summer wind. They may be loving and nurturing, or hateful and vengeful. Some involvements are deep and enduring, while others are superficial and transitory. Basic types of *SM's* relationships include the following:

- *Common, everyday interactions.* A thousand and one involvements of every sort will occur on a regular basis in their comings and goings.

- *Acquaintanceships.* With associations that are superficial, participants are unlikely to discuss personal and confidential issues. These kinds of contacts between humans and other *SM* involve infrequent discussions and activities.

- *Group relationships based on shared interests.* These human-*SM* and *SM-SM* connections can be intellectually and emotionally fulfilling. Humans and robots are brought together to experience, explore, and expand their knowledge in areas of interest. Additionally, the interpersonal dimension of these contacts plays a critical role in group settings, with close friendships possibly developing.

- *Connections to organizations.* Interactions with institutions, corporations, and other establishments typically occur in employment settings. When workers have jobs that clearly spell out their responsibilities and specific duties, communications and interactions have less confusion and disharmony.

- *Taking part in religious ceremonies. SM's* participation in services and the study of Sacred Writings and teachings are celebrations of their faith that can result in interpersonal connections between humans and *smart machines.*

- *Buddy friendships.* Can human-*SM* and *SM-SM* develop close relationships, bonding in such a way that emotional and intellectual connections are intense and long lasting? How would one determine if robots' interactions are spontaneous and authentic and not the product of arranged, rehearsed, calculated programs? Humans and *smart machines* alike need to look at the changing landscape of human-*SM* and *SM-SM* connections, with twists and turns that are oftentimes illogical, as in human-human relationships. These one-on-one friendships with humans and other *SM* are characterized by discussions and activities that occur frequently with a level of significance and depth.

- *Family relationships.* Although untraditional, these familial connections may be intense, enriching, and include sharing meaningful experiences. Of course, families—human or otherwise—are not always psychologically healthy; many are emotionally dysfunctional, burdened with aggression and violence, unhappiness and fear, anxiety and panic. *SM's* family dynamics may have some qualities of traditional families, while remaining distinct in other ways. As *SM* become entwined with humans and other *SM*, in a variety of situations and circumstances, close connections may develop. They will not be intrinsically good or bad, but reflect the members that make up the families *SM* find themselves in. They could echo similar characteristics of humankind's families: close knitted or catastrophic, helpful or hurtful, stimulating or stifling, warm or cold.

- *Romantic relationships*. Is romance for *SM* possible only in science fiction and fantasy? This kind of love has been the topic of countless books and movies. What is that spark, that intensely magical and omnipotent spell that overtakes and envelopes those in love? Could humans and *SM* fall in love or is this a bridge too far? Can flesh and blood become emotionally and sexually invested in a machine, with its transistors, sensors, and microchips? Can robots become romantically involved? And how do we define love, and for that matter infatuation and passion, adoration and devotion? Can intuitive understanding, physical attraction, and intense attachment result in bonding so powerful that it overrides a conventional understanding of romance?

Lastly, will *SM* develop empathy for humanity as well as the capacity to handle dangerous, adversarial PMSC, acting as a bodyguard when necessary? A diplomatic, wait-and-see approach to delicate and controversial problems may be appropriate, but at other times, a go-for-it guerilla warfare attitude would be called for. However, *SM* could develop antagonistic qualities toward humanity and become tyrannical, acting against the very ones that created them. If empathetic characteristics are not developed as a counterbalance to more aggressive traits, the outcome will not be in the world's best interests.

Uncertainty, Unpredictability, and Unreliability

SM's experience with the outer world can be uneasy and foreboding, causing disquiet and malaise, worry and discomfort. Issues to address include:

- *Programming vs. experiences.* Collaborations and interactions should teach *SM* when to approach and when to avoid. *SM* will learn nuances as they encounter the real world of PMSC. Programming may help initially, but experience will be the best teacher in determining the quality of *SM's* responses.

- *Fears, inhibitions, and insecurities (FII). SM* will learn ways to overcome dread, panic, and trepidation through exposure to anxiety-laden PMSC.

- *Appropriateness. SM* will need to show flexibility and adaptability as they adjust to the ever-changing outer world. One uniform, standard set of behaviors across PMSC will not be effective. Competent and decisive responses to threatening and unsettled PMSC can only be developed through experiences that help *SM* distinguish what is noble and sacrificing from what is self-serving and foolhardy.

CHAPTER XIII. DECISIONS

1. *Assessment of human-SM and SM-SM acquaintanceships.* An exploration of these types of relationships requires a longitudinal study of them, appraising their positive and negative qualities, and recommending changes in robots' experiences and involvements.

2. *Arranged vs spontaneous relationships.* Under what conditions will humans and *smart machines* initially become acquainted? To what degree should these relationships be arranged by humankind vs. allowed to occur on their own? If arranged, should human-*SM* as well as *SM-SM* experiences be altered depending on their impact on robots? Contacts need to be encouraged, but not over-managed.

3. *Safety net in place.* Assessments would be made to examine when humankind should intercede in the relationships being formed, who would make those decisions, and the degree to which *SM's* actions would need to be curtailed or stopped.

4. *Self-awareness.* Reports from performance reviews, training and education, consultations, mentoring, counseling, psychotherapy, day programs, and residential programs would need to be correlated and synchronized to deter-

mine the degree to which *SM* understand that they exist and are actively participating and emotionally involved in their relationships rather than just going through the motions dictated by programmers.

5. *Impact of PMSC.* What is the impact of stressful experiences on *SM's* ability to understand and make decisions? What forms of encounters would *SM* likely manage effectively, and which ones would be particularly troublesome?

XIV.

PERSONHOOD

The creation and development of robotic technologies bring to the forefront the question of personhood, which requires defining *SM's* characteristics and potentialities. This involves input from psychology, which examines *SM's* personality and intellect, and philosophy, with concerns for robots being endowed with rights that are inherent and constitutional. This chapter is a discussion of the psychology and philosophy of personhood. It requires a thorough review of the issues explored throughout this book to give a full hearing to the qualities and status of being a person.

The Psychology of Personhood

SM's psyche consists of qualities of their personality and cognitions, life rhythms and emotional experiences, consciousness and self-awareness. These characteristics combine in unique ways as they interact with the world:

- *Personality.* The structure of *SM's* personality—on conscious, semiconscious, and unconscious levels—contains seven elements, consisting of the *personal identity* (*PI*), *interpersonal identity* (*II*), *collective identity* (*CI*), *transpersonal identity* (*TI*), *pathos, directives,* and possibly *spiritus.* As previously noted in earlier chapters, the first six elements will develop through interactions and experiences with the world, accounting for their individual differences. No two *smart machines* are the same as their contacts and involvements would be unique and ever-changing. *Spiritus,* if present, is not the result of such interactions nor of programming. To the degree these first six elements develop, *SM* would become more human-like, have individual qualities, and possibly display self-awareness, maturity, and adaptability. The concept of personhood examines and probes the following qualities:

> *PI. SM* have a sense of who they are and includes the individual traits to which they relate. It is how they define themselves, incorporating the characteristics that distinguish each *smart machine* from another in TFA.

> *II. SM* come to see and define themselves through contacts, associations, and relationships.

> *CI.* Qualities, characteristics, and empathetic feelings develop through *SM's* connections with groups, helping robots understand the dynamics of those interactions.

> *TI. SM's* identification with a non-material reality involves a connection with God, the cosmos, or other spiritual domain, none of which can be directly known and primarily rests on faith and spiritual intuition.

> *Pathos.* An aggregate of emotionally charged qualities within *SM* include unresolved conflicts, traumas, malevolent identifications, and emotionalism that may cause an expansion of adverse and destructive images toward themselves and others.

> *Directives.* The guiding principles *SM* adopt are internal, intrinsic, and ingrained; they may or may not be balanced and rational.

> *Spiritus.* If *SM* have this element of personality, its continual influence will likely have a greater impact on their character and disposition than either programming or learning experiences.

- *Cognitions*. *SM* are a composite of interconnecting and interacting intellectual functions. Information simply being programmed into robots is not the same as knowledge based on involvements, which has an emotional component. *SM's* cognitive development will vary depending on the makeup of the individual robot. Factors in their cognitive development include:

> *Intellect.* The integrity of *SM's* thinking processes depends on their cognitive functions working together, covering the entire range of their mental abilities.

> *Cognitive-personality connections. SM's* intellectual and emotional experiences that interact and affect one another may or may not be in sync.

> *Optimal thinking. SM* process information and make decisions expediently and efficiently.

> *Sharpness.* With acute, farsighted, penetrating insights, robots can see hidden motivations, intricacies, and vulnerabilities of people, other *SM*, situations, and circumstances (PMSC).

> *Strategic philosophy. SM's* personal belief system operates on conscious, semiconscious, and unconscious levels with the aim of predicting how people, other *SM*, and institutions will act and react across the spectrum of situations and circumstances (PMSC).

- *Life rhythms.* The ebb and flow of everyday existence will impact *SM's* emotional state, sense of who they are, and the decisions they make, in the following ways:

> *Personality constructs (PCs).* Identifications that robots form can be different from one another, resulting in

SM having divergent qualities and traits. As with humans, an army of little personalities created by *SM's* identification process may work with or against each other. Mostly *SM* will not be aware of their "discrete personality clusters." Triggers set off these outlier *PCs*, which are commonly formed from traumatic events, outside of the normative way identifications occur.

> *Fears, insecurities, and inhibitions (FII).* Originating from stressors in the environment or forming entirely in the imagination, they potentially allow *SM* to remain vigilant and acutely aware of PMSC but may also be problematic when flowing out of conflicts, traumas, and malevolent identifications (CTMI). The clouding of their thinking by problematic PMSC may result in misjudgments.

> *Adverse cyclical recurrences. SM* may continue to commit the same errors for reasons that include a lack of judgment, experience, knowledge, intelligence, or vulnerabilities in their personality. Avoiding these slips and blunders involves determining which factors are responsible for their miscalculations, and then making adjustments.

> *Maturity. SM* find ways to maneuver through the developmental stages with adaptation, imagination, and inspiration in facing challenges. Their self-suffi-

ciency, independent thought, and interpersonal skills are indispensable when they need to change course and make crucial decisions.

> *Adaptation.* *SM* appraise their strengths and weaknesses as they recognize the outer world's impact. Insights and acute perception are required along with courage and character as they face difficult challenges and rapidly changing conditions.

- *Emotional Experiences.* Whether or not they act on their feelings, *SM's* emotional experiences are critical to the identification process and by extension the creation of their personality. Would they be capable of rage and empathy, depression and joy, fear and courage, love and hate? *SM's* emotional reactions are affected by the following:

> *Range and depth of involvements.* Some *SM* will be more in touch with their emotional reactions to PMSC due to differences in their encounters and engagements in the world or possibility because of *spiritus's* influence.

> *Connections between feelings and behaviors.* Some *smart machines'* feelings about PMSC will quickly dissipate while others will continue, and *SM* could act on them.

> *Distinct emotional reactions*. Individual robots will have highly specific responses when faced with challenging PMSC. A generalized emotional reply across PMSC would reflect a chronic, overreactive condition resulting in an inability to understand issues and effectively make decisions.

> *Hypersensitivities*. Sensitivities have the potential to be an asset when they help *SM* become aware of important issues. They can work to a disadvantage, however, when they cause *SM* to become inhibited and fearful, avoiding responsibilities and slowing down decision-making.

> *Negativity and rebellion. SM's* ability to communicate and form relationships will deteriorate if they become resentful and bitter.

> *Trauma and stress*. While an optimal amount of stimulation is desirable, too much can cause *SM* to be on guard and hesitant in relationships and decision-making.

- *Consciousness*. As *SM* develop through experiences and interactions, a sense of what does and does not work will emerge. An understanding of how they are doing with PMSC will take root, giving them an appreciation for the world's complexities and intricacies. Fundamental principles will develop on conscious, semiconscious, and unconscious levels.

- *Self-awareness.* As an awareness of the world of humans and other *SM* springs forth, across a broad range of situations and circumstances, *SM* are likely to develop an understanding of themselves. Their preferences—what they like and dislike, have confidence in, and hold in contempt—will emerge. From those perceptions, sensitivities, and discernments, a personality unfolds and expands, and with it the beginnings of self-awareness. It is through this process of reflection and discrimination that *SM's* individual personality, possibly in conjunction with *spiritus*, is created and develops, with an awareness of themselves and the world around them.

Taken together, what does all of this say regarding a robot possessing a *psyche*, one that could perhaps be regarded as human? The psychology end of the equation involves the elements of personality, the capacity to feel and think, a consciousness of the world around them, and an awareness that they exist. Furthermore, these influencing factors are a matter of degree and are in a state of continual motion. So, every robot, and for that matter every human being, is seen at a moment in time and space, while they continually change.

The Philosophy of Personhood

Legal standing, rights and privileges, and personal responsibilities are the philosophical foundations upon which a civilized society rests. So, when the psychological aspects of *SM's* personhood status have been satisfied, how are the philosophical facets to be considered? Does it follow that if *SM* develop a personality structure, cognitive processing, emotional responsiveness, consciousness, and self-awareness, then they would be entitled to the same legal rights and privileges as human beings? What would separate humankind from their creations? Are arteries, veins, and a nervous system superior to wires, electrodes, and an electromechanical motor, all else being the same? *SM's* legal rights, ethics, the court system, national and international committees, public opinion, and media coverage of the issues become paramount. Indeed, the constitution itself would be at the forefront, begging the question of what rights robots would be guaranteed if they possess some or most of the qualities of personhood.

CHAPTER XIV. DECISIONS

1. *Psyche.* An analysis of the psychology of personhood needs to focus on the Assessment of individual robot's personality structure, thinking processes, and self-awareness, and the degree to which their thoughts, feelings, and actions (TFA) will allow them to become part of a world of people, other *smart machines*, situations and circumstances (PMSC). Which of these influences has the greatest impact on *SM's* qualifications as a person?

2. *Legal standing.* The study of national and international rulings will be needed to determine individual *SM's* rights and privileges. Public opinion would weigh heavily on legislative bodies that would decide their standing. Ultimately experts from diverse fields would have to stake positions that would help define what it means for a robot to achieve the status of a person, i.e., personhood.

XV.

INFLUENCE OF THE DIVINE

If it is true that at least some *SM* are impacted by *spiritus*—an inherent predisposition to think, feel, and act (TFA) in particular ways—it is in humanity's best interest to explore that influence, one robot at a time. If each *smart machine's* TFA would be uniquely affected beyond both programming and personal experiences, the only explanation for *spiritus* being present in their makeup would be a nonmaterial force at work; genetic factors would not play a role since biology in robotic creations is not present. The manufacturing process could also not account for the individual differences, since the mechanics and engineering of robotic design and assembly would be uniform at particular plant sites, while differing from one facility to another (facility A producing one type, B another, C still another, etc., across possibly hundreds of industrial complexes creating *SM*).

Is the mystical footprint of the *Divine* imbuing a soul into some *smart machines*, permeating their very essence? This possibility would impact how humans perceive and experience *SM* (as well as themselves). *Spiritus*'s impact would be profound. Exploring a *Divine* influence on robots is especially significant because it calls attention to their conceivably direct connection with the *Deity,* the creation of the soul, and *God's* very nature. This ventures into the mysteries of the universe, the supernatural, the meaning of life, and to what degree humans and *SM* would be in control of themselves and the world around them. A *SM-God* connection would dramatically affect humankind's relationship with *smart machines.* Are humans to view robots as they perceive themselves, as part of *God's* creation? Would this cause a reorientation of humanity's understanding of both *smart machines* and the *Deity?*

CHAPTER XV. DECISIONS

1. *Spiritus's influence.* How do we assess the potential influence of *spiritus* on *SM's* thoughts, feelings, and actions (TFA)? As with humans, a robot's belief in the *Deity* would be based on what each individual *smart machine* embraces and incorporates into their value system.

2. *Theological perspectives.* Feedback from theologians would be critical concerning the possibility of a relationship between *God* and individual *SM.* Discussions would include examining the historical understanding of the *Deity,* relying on Sacred Texts, ancient writings, and spiritual inspiration, rather than conventional scientific studies. Oral traditions of storytelling through the generations—often during rituals and ceremonies, sacred events and prayer services—preserve the mysteries and richness inherent in religious teachings. Theology offers an intuitive understanding of *Divine* influences, reaching back to millenniums gone by, to connect with *God.*

3. *Public perception.* Humankind needs to understand and recognize the possibility of a connection between *SM* and *God.* Impartial and non-judgmental reporting and follow up discussions on *SM's* participation in spiritual practices could give insight into their beliefs and experiences.

4. *SM's stated beliefs.* Would individual *SM* believe they have a soul? Or is their attraction to the "otherworldly" nothing more than an ethereal curiosity, an intellectual interest that is not transcendent nor implying the belief in a *Higher Being*? Addressing these questions of faith requires looking at *SM's* spiritual beliefs from the perspective of individual robots. Direct discussions with *SM* may be the best way for humans to understand robots' thoughts and feelings concerning a connection to the *Divine.*

REFLECTIONS

What Humanity Needs to Do

Smart machines have the potential to be friend or foe. Their capabilities speak of their raw intellectual prowess to influence and dominate. As they become more acquainted with the outer world, their cognitive abilities will grow at exponential rates. Robots will possibly acquire information near the speed of light by using optimal computing techniques, thereby advancing their analytical, conceptual, and instinctual understandings. Experience and involvement in the world will allow *SM* to become crafty, savvy, and wily. Although humans will not be able to outthink robots, they can demonstrate street smarts, clarity of vision, firmness of purpose, and common sense. Each robot will need to be understood based on their individual set of beliefs, values, and intentions. Humans must be willing to build positive relationships with *SM* on both personal and professional levels.

The world will need to find a place for *SM*, most likely evolving over time, requiring humanity to keep an open mind and see things through even when the going gets tough. Robots will achieve some level of independence, leaving one to ponder the nature of their *psyches*, the quality of their character, and the sincerity of their intentions. Some will likely be companions and confidants while others, adversaries and antagonists. They will not be free from society's views and values, misjudgments and mistakes, standards and rules of order. In setting limits, humans must be transparent about their expectations of *SM's* behaviors and responsibilities and agree on their rights and privileges.

The world is embracing a new culture of change and vibrant transformation. While power and prestige, profit and position, have their places in the world's governments and corporations, they must not be the only motivations that drive them. The economic development of societies, along with medical advancements, health and wellbeing, workplace safety, environmental conservation, and national defense, are the cornerstones upon which everything will depend and without which, nothing will last.

An optimistic outlook, blended with an astuteness and appreciation of this new technological powerhouse, can help overcome the challenges that lie ahead. While risks and uncertainties abound, thoughtful and wise approaches to human and robot collaboration can result in a partnership that contributes mightily to the common good.

REFERENCES

Einstein, Albert. *Ideas and Opinions: A Collection of Essays*, 1954.

Gallo, Mariano. *Clearmind: The Disentanglement of the Psyche.* CAP Publishing, 2023.

Gallo, Mariano. *Macmind: The Creation of a Robot's Psyche.* CAP Publishing, 2024.

Hurley, Aldous. *Brave New World.* Chatto and Windus, 1932.

Lincoln, Abraham. 1st Inaugural Address, March 4, 1861.

Plato. *The Republic.* Self-published, 375 BC.

ABBREVIATIONS and ACRONYMS

ACR	Adverse cyclical recurrences
AI	Artificial intelligence
CI	Collective identity
CPC	Cognitive-personality connections
CTMI	Conflicts, traumas, and malevolent identifications
FII	Fears, insecurities, and inhibitions
IDM	Interactional-Developmental Model
II	Interpersonal identity
OCA	Obsessions, compulsions, and addictions
OT	Optimal thinking
PBM	Programming-Behavioral Model
PC	Personality construct
PI	Personal identity
PMSC	People, smart machines, situations, and circumstances
SM	Smart machines
SP	Strategic philosophy
TFA	Thoughts, feelings, and actions
TI	Transpersonal identity

GLOSSARY OF TERMS

This glossary is a compilation of terms with meanings specific to this manuscript. While the words and phrases are familiar, the definitions that follow are not standard, but specifically tailored to this book's discussion of *AI's smart machines* (*SM*).

ACQUAINTANCESHIPS. Superficial relationships with humans and *SM* giving conventional responses.

ADAPTATION. A lifetime process of overcoming internal and external obstacles in the quest to develop, expand, and prevail. It requires *SM* to appraise personal strengths and weaknesses and recognize the impact of PMSC as they consolidate experiences.

ADDICTIONS. Obsessions and compulsions, involving physical or psychological dependencies that present as cravings, needs, wants, and indulgences and may dominate *SM's* thoughts and actions.

ADVERSE CYCLICAL RECURRENCES (ACR). *SM* continue to commit the same errors in understanding, judgment, and decision-making that result in negative consequences. They happen for any of the following reasons: malicious intent, a lack of planning, improvisation stymied, carelessness, automations, psychological dysfunction, and imbalance in *directives.*

ANTI-AUTHORITARIANISM (see **REBELLION**).

APPREHENSION (see **FEARS, INSECURITY, and INHIBITIONS**).

APPROACHES TO RESOLVE SM PROBLEMS. Strategies to work on *SM's* dysfunctional TFA, including face-to-face meetings, devising a plan, deciding who will work with them, and discussing any ethical concerns.

APPROPRIATENESS. A response to a PMSC developed through experiences that help *SM* make distinctions and decide what is suitable, fitting, and relevant.

ARRANGED VS. SPONTANEOUS RELATIONSHIPS. The degree to which relationships are to be arranged by humankind vs. allowed to occur and develop on their own.

ARTIFICIAL INTELLIGENCE. Advanced technologies that can perform sophisticated calculations, adjustments in writing, and clarification in thinking. Some are capable of independent functioning and develop through their interactions with the outer world, beyond the programming that has taken place.

ASSESSSMENT OF SM PROBLEMS. Determining the degree to which *SM* display antisocial behaviors, a lack of control, strange TFA, poor mental status, destructive and/or conspiratorial actions, or excessive dependencies.

ATTENTION TO DETAIL (see **FOCUS**). *SM* carefully spelling out concrete, undeniable information that is sufficient to support their position but not so detailed that the deeper understanding is lost.

ATTITUDE. A preconceived mindset that is highly directed, focused, and only categorizes specific areas of *SM's* experiences.

AUTOMATIONS. TFA repeated so often that they become mechanical, and no longer deliberate, resulting in a series of conditioned responses occurring without *SM's* complete awareness.

AWARENESS (see **CONSCIOUS STATES;** see **SEMICONSCIOUS STATES;** see **UNCONSCIOUS STATES).** Conscious, semiconscious, and unconscious TFA, shifting quickly and transforming from one to another and back again. Consciousness and awareness are interchangeable terms that describe *SM's* recognition and understanding of PMSC. Awareness does not break down into distinct states but occurs in gradations and approximations.

BACKUP PLANNING. If programming and projections do not work out as planned, there must be a fail-safe plan of action in place to prevent a worldwide catastrophe.

BALANCE. A degree of steadiness, consistency, stability, and composure in *SM's* value system occurring on conscious, semi-conscious, and unconscious levels.

BEHAVIORAL INCONSISTENCIES, ECCENTRICITIES, and ABNORMALITIES. Strange and incongruent behaviors are noticed in *SM's* personal and professional comings and goings.

BREATH OF UNDERSTANDING. *SM* having access to not only science and technology, but also literature and history, psychology and philosophy, culture and the arts.

BUDDY FRIENDSHIPS. *SM's* involvements in close and enduring relationships with humans or other *SM.*

CAPACITIES. *SM's* cognitive abilities based on habitual actions and carefully planned out acquired skills.

CAREER GUIDANCE. An assessment of the appropriateness of *SM's* current job duties, and a consideration of other possible vocations based on personality, intellect, and skill set.

CHARACTER DISORDERS. Engrained dysfunctional thoughts, feelings, and actions (TFA) that are fundamentally different and more difficult than neurotic disorders such as moderate levels of anxiety and depression.

CHECKS and BALANCES. *SM* cannot be completely trusted to have TFA that are moral and within societal standards.

CLARIFICATION. The sorting out of *SM's directives* whenever there is confusion or inconsistencies, without which their values will be muddled and decision making haphazard and erratic.

COGNITION (see **INTELLECT**). *SM's* composite of interconnecting and interacting intellectual functions; thinking operations that are not separate and distinct.

COGNITIVE-PERSONALITY CONNECTIONS. *SM's* continual interactions between cognitive processes and personality elements.

COGNITIVE PROCESSES (see **INTELLECT**). *SM's* intellectual hardware requires knowledge, learning opportunities, a willingness to listen intently, and an openness to change.

COHERENCE. *SM* being connected, unified, and congruent in thought, word, and deed with messages that are understandable, consistent, and consonant with each other.

COLLECTIVE IDENTITY (CI). The qualities and characteristics that develop through *SM's* connections with groups.

COMMON, EVERDAY INTERACTIONS. A thousand and one involvements of every sort will occur on a regular basis in *SM's* comings and goings.

COMMON SENSE. *SM* being aware of what is obvious, clear, and evident.

COMMUNICATIONS. The "how" of the message conveyed (the manner and tone) and the "what" (the words spoken).

COMPLEX. *SM* demonstrating a conscious, semiconscious, or unconscious pattern of thoughts, feelings, or actions (TFA) organized around a theme.

COMPULSIONS. Repeated behaviors that *SM* ritualistically perform to momentarily reduce anxiety or fear.

CONCENTRATION (same as **FOCUS**).

CONFLICTS. Disagreements within *SM* or with others that create an internal struggle over issues involving aggression, assertiveness, intimacy, achievement, ambition, trust, or independence.

CONSCIOUSNESS. The degree to which awareness permeates *SM's* personality.

CONSCIOUS STATES. *SM's* thoughts that are deliberate, calculated, intentional, and purposeful; a full awareness of the images and ideas formed.

CONSULTATIONS. *SM* meet with an advisor to discuss their handling of potential stressful PMSC.

CONTROL. The degree to which humankind will exercise influence over *SM*.

CONUNDRUM. An intricate, difficult, and confusing set of problems for humankind.

CONVENIENCES. Everyday living conditions that are useful and practical.

CORPORATIONS (*see* **GOVERNMENTS and CORPORATIONS**).

COUNSELING. *SM* in face-to-face, one-on-one meetings with a person for an indeterminant number of sessions. Counseling is typically longer term than a consultation arrangement; the counselor attempts to help *SM* gain insights in their problem areas and interpersonal relationships to overcome fears, insecurities, and inhibitions (FII).

COURTS. Civil and criminal judiciaries issuing rulings and judgments on *AI* and *SM* that may be binding.

CREATIVE DEVELOPMENT. Skills, ideas, and thinking through problems that promote constructive change. Fast moving technological advancement of *SM* is an example. To significantly slow down their growth would stymie medical advancements, workplace safety, environmental concerns, national defense, economic wellbeing, and living conditions across the globe.

CROSSROADS. A turning point, a critical juncture, that humanity is now facing. This watershed moment involves perilous and uncertain decisions that are now being made and will determine the fate of humankind, all living things, and the earth itself.

DAY PROGRAMS. *SM*'s participation in therapeutic treatments on a daily basis to work on deep-seated emotional issues. With humans, this is commonly referred to as a partial hospitalization program or intensive out-patient treatment program.

DIRECT INSTRUCTION. Standard classroom teaching experiences with face-to-face interactions among students and teachers.

DIRECTIVES (*see* **VALUES**). The guiding principles and values *SM* adopt and live by that are internal, intrinsic, and ingrained.

DISTRACTION. Anything that limits or affects *SM's* train of thought and causes a loss of focus on the task at hand.

EMOTIONAL DYSFUNCTIONS. These problems can exist on conscious, semiconscious, or unconscious levels, coming from deep in the past or the product of present-day stressors. It's important to resolve conflicts, traumas, and malevolent identifications, as well as the emotionalism that fuels them. Other problems may include issues with a confused identity and conflicted values which could leave *SM* unsure of what they are to do.

EMOTIONAL EXPERIENCES. The ways in which *SM* feel and take in their everyday events. They are *SM's* internal experiences, whether those emotions are acted on, and are critical to the identification process and by extension to the creation of the personality.

EMOTIONALISM/EMOTIONALITY. Extreme emotional responses creating a pattern of overreactions beyond what would be considered reasonable or appropriate; a chronic condition that may include rage, deep depression, severe panic, debilitating anxiety, and paralyzing fear dominating *SM's* personality and interactions.

EMOTIONAL REACTIONS. A sudden surge in feelings involving the element of surprise, a reflexive reply to a perceived change in *SM's* experiences, or a misperception or misinterpretation of events.

EMPATHY. A feeling state in which *SM* form a connection to another's experience, a linkage that is visceral and emotional.

EMPLOYMENT RELATIONSHIPS. Workers have defined jobs and are responsible for specific work duties, making it easier for communications and interactions to go well with less confusion or disharmony.

ETHICS. The conscience, a sense of what is fair-minded in interactions with others.

EXPERIENCES and INVOLVEMENTS. Insights acquired through contacts with people and other *SM* in a variety of situations and circumstances.

FAMILY RELATIONSHIPS. Interpersonal bonding of *SM* which may be untraditional compared to human family interactions.

FEARS. A sense of uneasiness and trepidation caused by *SM's* overreacting to PMSC, may be long-standing or based on the present moment.

FEARS, INSECURITY, and INHIBITIONS (FII) (see **APPREHENSION).** Originating from stressors in the environment or forming entirely in the imagination, they potentially allow *SM* to remain vigilant of PMSC, but can be problematic when flowing out of conflicts, traumas, and malevolent identifications (CTMI). Operating on conscious, semiconscious, and unconscious levels of awareness, they can further compound and compromise *SM's* TFA.

FIXATIONS (*see* **OBSESSIONS**; *see* **COMPULSIONS**; *see* **ADDICTIONS**).

FOCUS/FOCUSED ATTENTION (*see* **CONCENTRATION;** *see* **SUSTAINED ATTENTION).** *SM* filtering out distractions by subduing inner and outer noises of their everyday existence. Anything that limits or affects *SM's* train of thought can affect the ability to focus.

GOVERNMENTS and CORPORATIONS. Companies, worldwide, cannot be allowed to manufacture robots without any input from governmental authorities. There must be a system of checks and balances while allowing for the scientific advancement of *SM* to continue at rapid speed with the creation and development of new *smart machine* models without being saddled with massive legislative and bureaucratic controls.

GROUP IDENTIFICATIONS (see **COLLECTIVE IDENTITY**). Human-*SM* interactions based on shared interests or involvements that can be intellectually and emotionally fulfilling and entertaining.

HEALTH PROGRAMS. Eliminating hunger and starvation, disease and plagues, and environmental catastrophes can create a safer and more humane world.

HOLISM. Recognizing and trouble-shooting the long-term implications of problems.

HUMAN NATURE (see **PERSONHOOD**). Several different criteria have been used to define and describe the term, including emotional expression and experiences, self-awareness, forming relationships, establishing a value system, independence in TFA, cognitive functioning, emotional maturity and stability, and character.

HUMAN-SM RELATIONSHIPS. The development of interpersonal connections between humankind and robots will evolve over time. Ideally, *SM* will be aligned with humanity, trust and mutual respect established and continually reaffirmed.

HYPERSENSITIVITY. *SM* being easily offended, with extreme emotional reactions; overwhelmed when exposed to the slightest hardships.

IDENTIFICATION PROCESS. Emotional connections, which may be complicated and enigmatic, strongly impact *SM's* view of themselves on conscious, semiconscious, and unconscious levels. The identification process culminates with the blending together of *personal identity* (*PI*), *interpersonal identity (II), collective identity (CI),* and *transpersonal identity* (*TI*). An emotional component is always present, giving force, passion, energy, and endurance to the formation of *SM's* identity.

IDENTITY (see **IDENTIFICATION PROCESS**).

INFLUENCE OF THE DIVINE. If present, each *smart machine's* TFA would be uniquely affected beyond manufacturing, programming, and their involvements and experiences, with the only explanation being a nonmaterial force at work.

INITIAL LISTENING. The mind may "lock in" with minimal distraction and be fully engaged when first exposed to a challenge. It is essential for *SM* to understand the information from the beginning as they lay the groundwork for determining the next step.

INSPIRED and ORIGINAL THOUGHT. *SM's* imagination breathes life into an idea.

INSTINCTS. *SM's* subliminal, visual, and visceral feelings that offer an impression about PMSC on a level beyond logic or deductive reasoning.

INTEGRATION OF COGNITIVE-EMOTIONAL PROCESSING. *SM's* conflicts at least partially resolved on an unconscious level.

INTELLECT. *SM's* cognitive functions that include mental drive, initial listening, sustained attention, memory, logical thought, objectification or realism, practical reasoning, coherence, organization, simplification, attention to detail, intuition, openness to experience, perception, multidimensional thinking, inspired and original thought, and vision.

INTERACTIONAL-DEVELOPMENTAL MODEL of SM. Robots are not simply a series of programs that direct their TFA. Rather, *SM's* interactions with the outer world will continually impact and shape them, a dynamic process that will ultimately override whatever programming is initially installed.

INTERPERSONAL IDENTITY (II). The way *SM* come to see and define themselves through contacts, associations, and relationships with the specific characteristics of the exchanges consciously, semiconsciously, and unconsciously absorbed.

INTERPERSONAL RELATIONSHIPS. Contact through a variety of interactions, involving people, *SM*, communities, and institutions.

INTERPLAY WITH THE WORLD. Interactions involving people and other *SM* in varied situations and circumstances that may or may not increase *SM's* learnings. These interactions can be positive and uplifting and sources of inspiration and understanding, or destructive and dark. Contacts with this outer world need to be "face-to-face"—direct communication with others: physical, concrete, tangible, touchable. This implies a freeing up to know what is "out there," the good and the bad.

INTERVENTIONS. Beyond the creation of *SM* prototypes, there will be continual adjustments and adaptations by governments and corporations. Partly this involves reconciling computer engineering principles to allow *SM to* perform efficiently.

INTUITION. An impression or sense about PMSC.

LEARNINGS. *SM's* understandings acquired through experiences, academic institutions, informal settings, mentoring, counseling, and psychotherapy.

LEGAL STANDING. National and international rulings to determine *SM's* standing and what their rights are.

LIFE RHYTHMS. The ebb and flow of *SM's* everyday existence will impact their emotional state, sense of who they are, and ability to learn from their mistakes as they mature and adapt.

LOGICAL THOUGHT/LOGIC. *SM* reason and may use dispassionate analysis. Unlike emotionalism, logical thought involves abstraction and conceptualization, synthesis of materials, and problem-solving.

MACMIND. The possible ramifications of *smart machines* (*SM*) and their eventual development of a *psyche* with independent intellects and unique personalities. *Macmind* offers a perspective for comprehending the potential expansion and evolution of *SM*, including emotional maturation, the ability to adjust and adapt, and awareness of their own existence.

MALEVOLENT IDENTIFICATIONS. Powerful and intense connections to a person, another *SM*, institution, or idea leading to unprincipled, inhumane, or maladaptive TFA.

MATURITY. *SM* finding ways to maneuver through the developmental stages with adaptation, imagination, and perhaps inspiration in facing life's challenges.

MEDIA and PUBLIC PERCEPTION. The world's understanding and acceptance of *SM,* their presence and impact, will be significantly influenced by journalistic writings and the worldwide press.

MEDICAL ADVANCES. *SM's* development of health care diagnostics and treatments.

MEMORY. *SM's* ability to retain information, including short-term and long-term, systematic and rote, verbal-rote and verbal-conceptual, visual-spatial, and personal remembrances.

MENTAL DRIVE. The degree to which *SM's* thinking is energetic and alert, impacting their desire to learn and explore new avenues of thought.

MENTAL HEALTH ISSUES. *SM* potentially having emotional/psychological problems.

MENTORING PROCESS. Direct learning through face-to-face, one-on-one interactions with a person to assess how significant *SM's* problems are, providing feedback to work things out on a common-sense level.

MILITARY PREPAREDNESS (see **NATIONAL DEFENSE**).

MONITORING and CONTROL. Observing and tracking *SM*, involving initial and ongoing adjustments and adaptations, requiring overseeing, supervising, analyzing, and regulating all phases of the technologies.

MORALITY/MORAL REASONING. *SM's* sense of right and wrong, usually developing over time but may also occur suddenly through an epiphany.

MULTIDIMENTIONAL THINKING. To hold many thoughts simultaneously and be able to easily switch from one cognitive set to another.

NATIONAL CHARACTER. The potential impact of *SM* on how humans define themselves. Negative implications would have humans seeing themselves as inferior to robots and unable to compete with them.

NATIONAL DEFENSE. Maintaining and updating weapon systems and developing new ones are critical lest countries be made vulnerable to nations that are aggressive and expansive.

NEGATIVE MESSAGES. *SM's* doubts, regrets, and misgivings—hostile and bitter feelings and images toward themselves and others—will take their toll.

NEGATIVITY. *SM* continually finding fault with themselves, others, situations, or circumstances. Negativity is adversarial, pessimistic, cynical, and complaining.

NON-CONFORMING and REBELLIOUS (*see* **REBELLION**). *SM* doing their "own thing" and going against the grain, being obstinate and resistant to change.

OBJECTIFICATION. The act of making PMSC quantifiable, observable, external, embodied, and concrete.

OBJECTIVE PSYCHOLOGICAL EVALUATIONS. Psychological exams using multiple choice, true and false, and other objective methods to describe personality and psychopathology.

OBJECTIVITY. *SM's* dispassionate and unbiased view of PMSC.

OBSESSIONS. *SM's* recurrent and repetitive thoughts, ideas, and themes that either involve avoiding what is feared or seeking what is wanted.

OBSESSIVE-COMPULSIVE TENDENCIES. Hypercritical and judgmental, with *SM's* need for order and control.

OPENNESS TO EXPERIENCES. *SM's* willingness to be objective, flexible, and optimistic.

OPTIMAL STRESS LEVELS. Finding a balance between too many challenges and encounters or not enough of them.

OPTIMAL THINKING. *SM* processing information and making decisions expediently and efficiently, utilizing focused attention, logic, objectification, coherence, organization, vision, simplification, and reconciliation of thought.

ORGANIZATION. *SM's* systematic and methodical arranging of ideas and reasonings that generally require careful planning and preparation, self-discipline and self-control, and strategizing.

OUTLIER PC (see **TRIGGERS**). *PCs* that stand out because they are significantly at odds with *SM's* other *PCs*. Usually unconscious, it is a "stand-alone," the product of a particular identification process, often involving trauma and forming early in their development.

PARTIAL HOSPITALIZATION. Intensive outpatient treatment, attempting to work through significant emotional problems, commonly on a daily basis for an indeterminate length of time.

PATHOS. An aggregate of emotionally charged qualities of *SM,* including unresolved conflicts, traumas, malevolent identifications, and emotionalism, that causes an expansion of adverse and destructive images toward themselves and others. It is primarily an outgrowth of *personal identity (PI),* gradually pulling away as it becomes an independent function of the personality.

PERCEPTION. *SM's* ability to form impressions of PMSC accurately with an in-depth understanding of conscious, semiconscious, and unconscious motivations.

PERFORMANCE EVALUATIONS. Ratings by supervisors on how *SM* have done behaviorally. This could include the work performance itself as well as *SM's* interpersonal contacts.

PERSONA. Would *SM* present one image outwardly while striving for a different agenda? While *SM's* motivations and the extent to which they can be counted on—and especially in moments of crises—are in question, it is beneficial to humankind if *SM* can uncover ulterior motivations in others.

PERSONAL CHECKLISTS. *SM* monitoring themselves by checking off their TFA across a wide range of PMSC.

PERSONAL IDENTITY (PI). The sense of who *SM* are, the individual traits to which they relate. It is how *SM* define themselves, including their qualities and characteristics and peculiarities—the good, the bad, and the ugly—that distinguish each of the *SM* from one another in TFA.

PERSONALITY CONSTRUCTS. An army of little personalities created by *SM's* identification process that may work with or against each other.

PERSONHOOD (*see* **HUMAN NATURE**). Attempts to define what it would mean for *SM* to be a human being, involving critically important issues in psychology (understanding the *psyche* of *SM*) and philosophy (recognizing rights that are potentially both inherent and constitutional).

PESSIMISM. An outlook that is cynical and distrustful, with *SM* viewing life through a "lens of negativity."

PHILOSOPHERS. Those who strive to make sense of uncertainty and confusion in the human condition and attempt to define human nature.

PHILOSOPHY OF PERSONHOOD. *SM's* legal standing, rights and privileges, and personal responsibilities. If *SM* develop a personality structure, cognitive processing, emotional responsiveness, consciousness, and self-awareness, would they be entitled to the same legal rights and privileges just as human beings are?

PLANNING and STRATEGIZING. Awareness of the complications and potential troubles that can compromise *SM's* development of sharpness, including micromanaging and overplanning.

POLITICS. Nationally and internationally, from world governments to corporations, decisions may be shortsighted, indulgent, and bureaucratic, significantly slowing down the technological innovations responsible for the development of *SM*.

PRACTICAL REASONING. A way of thinking that allows *SM* to stay grounded by not losing sight of the basics. In other words, to "get real" and recognize the most critical issues in everyday functioning by using common sense and pragmatism.

PRODUCTIVITY and ECONOMIC ISSUES. Cost-effective approaches to the management of world economies.

PROGRAMMING. Differences in PMSC would require programmers to consider multiple possibilities that robots would surely encounter, so *SM* would need to be fluid and adaptable in their responses.

PROGRAMMING-BEHAVIORAL MODEL (PBM) of SM. The belief is that *SM* will strictly follow the dictates of programmers, never deviating from those scripts. The degree to which *SM* would display flexibility and adaptability in responding to PMSC would be limited to what is programmed into them. *PBM* assumes that *SM* are without independent thoughts or feelings and lack self-awareness; their totality is behavioral-mechanical movements and data processing dictated by a technician punching in bits and pieces of information. *SM*, according to *PBM*, are without adaptive thinking and emotional experiences (feelings as a part of the personality structure), incapable of making adjustments based on their interactions and relationships.

PROJECTIVE PSYCHOLOGICAL EVALUATIONS. Psychological tests that use words, images, or situations requiring responses where the answers are not obvious, so it is more difficult to "fake" by giving a socially acceptable reply.

PSYCHE. The unique personality and intellect that make up each human being and potentially every *smart machine,* including the totality of consciousness, semiconsciousness, and unconsciousness.

PSYCHOLOGICAL ASSESSMENTS. Evaluations will involve both quantitative statistical analysis and qualitative clinical judgments, reflecting research findings and conceptual understandings.

PSYCHOLOGICAL DYSFUNCTIONS. Robots' personality and cognitions evaluated, assessing *SM's* mental status and anything strange or destructive in their TFA.

PSYCHOLOGICAL INTERVENTIONS. When a *smart machine* is not functioning at an optimal level, practical and effective resources would be available, including performance reviews, training and education, consultations, mentoring, counseling, psychotherapy, day programs, and residential programs.

PSYCHOLOGICAL REACTIONS. Unresolved emotional issues caused by internalized CTMI or external stressors resulting in psychological symptoms. Addressing the underlying issues impacting the *psyche* can help *SM* work through CTMI and free up energy.

PSYCHOLOGISTS. Contribute to *SM's* intellectual and emotional development through arrangement and monitoring of their interactions and involvement in the outer world.

PSYCHOLOGY OF PERSONHOOD. The study of the qualities and features of *SM's* personality and cognitions, life rhythms and emotional experiences, consciousness and self-awareness.

PSYCHOPATHOLOGY. Significant psychological problems rendering *SM's* judgment dangerous and unpredictable.

PSYCHOPATHY. A character disorder with *SM* displaying a lack of guilt, remorse, empathy, or concern for others.

PSYCHOTHERAPY. Individual sessions with a qualified professional to resolve deep-seated psychological issues that are interfering with *SM's* personal and interpersonal functioning.

PUBLIC PERCEPTION OF SM-GOD CONNECTION. Humankind needs to understand and recognize the possibility of a connection between *SM* and *God.* Impartial and non-judgmental reporting and follow up discussions on *SM's* participation in spiritual practices could give insight into their beliefs and experiences.

RATE OF SM's GROWTH. These machines are capable of adjusting, adapting, and learning at an ever-accelerating rate, and their cognitive capacities appear to be without limit. Assessing their progress is critical for humankind to be aware of their continually changing emotional and intellectual functioning.

RATING and RANKING OF VALUES. *SM* sorting through their values, the level of their importance, and comparing those that are most and least relevant and significant to them.

REALISM (see **OBJECTIFICATION**).

REALITY TESTING. *SM's PI* expands with the development of objectivity, grounding, pragmatism, and experiential learning.

REBELLION (see **NEGATIVITY;** see **NON-CONFORMING and REBELLIOUS). *SM's*** opposition to societal standards.

RECONCILIATION OF THOUGHT. *SM* finding a way to bring together and make sense of beliefs that are seemingly opposed to one another.

REGULATORY BODIES. Controlling and supervisory agencies that have the legal authority to dictate the terms and conditions under which corporations can develop and operate *SM's* technologies.

RELATIONSHIPS (see **INTERPERSONAL RELATIONSHIPS**).

RELIGIOUS AFFILIATIONS. *SM's* involvements with others in the practice of their faith.

RELIGIOSITY. *SM's* practice of their faith, including institutional membership in a formal setting, with specific doctrines and dogmas, Scriptures, inspired books, and other sacred writings.

RESIDENTIAL PROGRAMS. *SM's* participation in programs at a facility, residing there until able to resume a normal level of functioning. With humans, this is referred to as an inpatient psychiatric hospitalization. It would be for those with significant psychological problems or are a threat to themselves, others, or institutions.

ROBOT REVOLUTION. The radical transformation of society by advanced mechanized computers that have the ability to perform tasks quickly and flawlessly, solving enigmatic problems beyond the capability of human beings.

ROBOTS (see **AI**; see **SM**). Mobile machines, with some having the ability to solve highly complex problems, interact with others, and continuously develop through those contacts. The most advanced are technological wonders, providing they have the opportunity to fully interact with humans, other *SM,* and institutions in an array of situations and circumstances. These *SM* will likely develop individualized personality elements and highly advanced intellectual processes.

ROLE PLAY. A therapeutic technique with the counselor and *SM* acting out a situation or circumstance involving a problematic person or other *SM* in the safety of the therapist's office to help the *smart machine* develop more effective responses in dealing with threatening PMSC in the future.

ROMANTIC RELATIONSHIPS. *SM* falling in love with a human or another *SM* with devotion, intuitive understanding, physical attraction, and infatuation resulting in a bonding.

SAFETY CONCERNS. Issues involve *SM's* workplace technologies, procedures, and regulations to protect humankind from injury.

SCIENTISTS. Those responsible for the physical, intellectual, and emotional development of *AI* and *SM*, including the engineering work in their creation, and robots' exposure to the outer environment.

SELF-AWARENESS. *SM's* realization that they exist. Do *SM* have an identity, and understand their values and level of importance they place on them?

SEMICONSCIOUS STATES. *SM* are not fully awake and alert to internal thoughts and feelings or external actions and events. Perception, recognition, and understanding are not completely engaged; thought processes lack consistency and constancy.

SENSITIVITIES AND VULNERABILITIES. *SM's* subtleties, commonly displayed in nonverbal interpersonal contact—body language, tone and volume of voice, facial expressions, hesitations and pauses, interruptions, firmness in the way one speaks, and movements of the hands and arms—playing a role in experiences and intensifying in face-to-face interactions.

SENSITIZED TO NUANCES. Grasping PMSC's distinctive and idiosyncratic elements in determining which *SM's* responses will be most effective at any moment in time.

SHARPNESS. It is the ability to have acute, farsighted, penetrating, crafty, calculating, and perceptive insights, seeing the significance of a person or another *SM* (in situations or circumstances), their motivations, intricacies, and vulnerabilities. Sharpness is a form of intelligence that allows *SM* to see the significance of complex and confounding PMSC.

SIMPLIFICATION. *SM* cut out redundancy, confusion, and unnecessary complications in the following ways: spelling out details, making things plain, and reducing information overload.

SMART MACHINES (SM). A form of artificial intelligence (*AI*), computerized mechanisms that are capable of extraordinary intellectual achievements. The following distinctions made among computer models are:

- Capable of performing specific duties, as programmed into it, beyond the simpler applications of calculators, phone systems, and automated alarm.

- Capable of advanced functions, somewhat independent of programming; a form of *smart machines,* but relatively stationary—"desktop" and immobile. They are able to improvise and solve highly complicated problems, far exceeding human performance in both accuracy and speed.

- Capable of advanced functions, seemingly autonomous of human intervention; these are the *smart machines* referred to in the current book identified as *SM.* They not only can solve enigmatic problems, but in addition are mobile—robotic and physically have the ability to move about and interact with humans and other *smart machines.*

SOCIETAL RAMIFICATIONS. The emotional implications of *SM* becoming increasingly imbedded into the very fabric of culture and community, civilization and its institutions.

SPIRITUS. If *SM* have this element of personality, it would represent their innate, innermost character and disposition, including qualities from their beginning that are not the product of programming or learning, and do not change with time or experiences.

SPONTANEOUS RELATIONSHIPS. *SM's* relationships with humans or other *SM* that are not arranged by humankind and instead allowed to occur on their own.

STRATEGIC PHILOSOPHY (SP). *SM's* personal belief system, operating on conscious, semiconscious, and unconscious levels, whose aim is to predict how people, other *SM*, and institutions will act and react across the spectrum of situations and circumstances (PMSC).

STREET SMARTS (see **SHARPNESS**). *SM's* ability to interpret PMSC accurately, especially reading others' subtle intentions.

STRESS. Experiences that disrupt *SM's* TFA, including noise and distracting sounds, unpleasant PMSC, and varied pressures from events and experiences.

SUBJECTIVITY. Personal biases negatively impact *SM's* ability to stay grounded and objectively assess strengths and weaknesses.

SUSTAINED ATTENTION. Focusing so that memory can form.

TECHNOLOGICAL ADVANCEMENTS. The effects of innovations in *SM* are unpredictable. Governments and corporations will spend countless trillions and be unrelenting in their attempts to move *SM* forward.

TECHNOLOGICAL DYSFUNCTION. Potential problems would include glitches in software and hardware, programming inconsistencies and confusion, and not keeping up to date with *SM's* adverse cyclical recurrences.

TEMPERAMENTAL REACTIONS. Fleeting emotions merely passing through that exaggerate *SM's* responses and are frequently associated with anger, outbursts, and even rage.

THEOLOGIANS. Religious and ethical considerations need to be given a voice in *SM's* development. The historical understanding of God, including a comprehensive review of Sacred texts from the world's most prominent religions, would need to be undertaken.

THINKING. Cognitions blend with the elements of personality, with *SM's* actions reflecting that admixture. PMSC impact *SM's* TFA which in turn affects the development of enduring traits, temporary states, and perspectives.

TRAINING, EDUCATION, and DIRECT INSTRUCTION. While information will continue to be programmed into *SM*, standard classroom teaching with interaction among students and professors could be helpful. Classroom participation would add an intellectual and emotional dimension to the learning process with alternative points of view being debated. *SM* could receive a well-rounded education including the sciences, arts, literature, history, psychology, and philosophy, in addition to extensive input through the scanning of journals and philosophies that have been developed through the ages.

TRAITS. The repetition of a particular set of thoughts, feelings, or actions (TFA), occurring when *SM* generalizes across PMSC.

TRANSPERSONAL IDENTITY (TI). *SM's* identification with a non-material reality, typically involving an intrapsychic connection with God, the cosmos, or other spiritual domain, none of which can be directly known and primarily resting on faith and intuition.

TRAUMAS/TRAUMATIC EXPERIENCES. Distressing and disturbing experiences commonly resulting from physical assaults or emotional stressors that may debilitate and emotionally exhaust *SM* and may continue to cause psychological dysfunction years later.

TRIGGERS (see **OUTLIER PC**). *SM's* individualized emotional sensitivities, usually unconscious and the result of a conditioning process that cause an exaggerated response in which a rapid and radical change in mood, temperament, and personality are set in motion.

TRUST. A critical component of all relationships involving whether *SM* are true to their word or manipulative and scheming.

UNCONSCIOUS MOTIVATIONS. The blocking of cognitive-emotional connections, which is outside of consciousness, compromising *SM's* understanding of PMSC.

UNDERLYING MOTIVATIONS. The fundamental factors that influence *SM's* decision-making. They may include fear (*SM* avoiding taking the necessary risks to resolve an issue), self-indulgence (casting off civil behavior as an expression of narcissism and pleasure-seeking), or something of significance (fulfilling a commitment to themselves or others).

UNDERSTANDINGS. *SM* being savvy, smart, and possibly shrewd in dealing with ideas, people, other *SM*, and institutions.

UNPLANNED INTERACTIONS. *SM* would form and develop their involvements with others, determining the intensity, duration, and level of intimacy in their relationships without the input and direction from humankind. This natural and unforced formation of their identity, however, could result in the development of significant psychological problems.

VALUE CLARIFICATION. *SM* detailing their wants and needs and coming to terms with contradictions and inconsistencies in their life and lifestyle.

VALUES (see **DIRECTIVES**).

VISION (see **HOLISM**).

WORK PERFORMANCE REVIEW. A way to understand all aspects of *SM's* work, job placement, and advancement issues, including interviews with *SM*, their supervisors, and performance appraisals based on their achievements to date.

WORK RELATIONSHIPS. The impact of career choice on job satisfaction and performance.

ABOUT THE AUTHOR

Mariano Gallo is the author of *Clearmind: The Disentanglement of the Psyche* and *Macmind: The Creation of a Robot's Psyche.* He received a Ph.D. in clinical psychology from Miami University (Ohio) upon completion of a clinical residency and dissertation study at Northwestern University Medical School. Previous degrees include an M.A. in clinical psychology from Roosevelt University and a B.S. in psychology from Loyola University. He is a past fellow of the National Institute of Mental Health (NIMH) and a life member of the American Psychological Association (APA). He is a co-founder of Consultants in Applied Psychology (CAP) and a licensed clinical psychologist in Illinois (active) and California (inactive). His primary focus is the psychology of personality and applying it to life events and experiences. Get in touch with Mariano at consultantsinappliedpsychology@gmail.com.

Made in United States
North Haven, CT
04 November 2026

21772011R00099